DECO
DELIGHTS

Wimberly Allison Tong & Goo
Architects and Planners

2260 University Drive, Newport Beach, California 92660
Telephone 714 574 8500 Facsimile 714 574 8550

DECO DELIGHTS

Preserving the Beauty and Joy
of Miami Beach Architecture

Barbara Baer Capitman

Photographs by Steven Brooke

E. P. DUTTON   New York

About the Illustrations Appearing Before the Start of the Text

Page 2: A detail of the roof and wall of Friedman's Bakery—a delightful confection in blue, pink, green, and white at 485 Washington Avenue before it was repainted in black and gold and renamed Watergun. Another detail photograph of this building appears on page 61.

Page 8: This detail photograph of the front of the Imperial Hotel at 650 Ocean Drive highlights the handsome floral carving in the vertical green bands. The entire hotel is illustrated on page 15.

Page 9: The Imperial Hotel is graced by an imposing balustrade of abstract concrete forms made more significant by the paintwork.

Page 10: This detail photograph of the rich treatment of the walls of Your Everything Store at 659 Washington Avenue (illustrated on page 61) is a superb example of the way an imaginative palette contributes so effectively to the beauty of architectural detail.

Book design by Marilyn Rey

Published in the United States by E. P. Dutton, a division of Penguin Books USA Inc., 2 Park Avenue, New York, N.Y. 10016. / Published simultaneously in Canada by Fitzhenry and Whiteside Limited, Toronto. / Library of Congress Catalog Card Number: 88-71759. / Printed and bound by Dai Nippon Printing Co., Hong Kong, Ltd. / ISBN: 0-525-48381-0.
20 19 18 17 16 15 14

The Senator—Symbol of the Deco District

In the spring of 1988 thousands of Miamians drove to the Senator Hotel—at 1201 Collins Avenue and designed by L. Murray Dixon in 1939—to assure themselves that the hotel was still standing, for it had become a beautiful mute symbol of District success. The owners, possessing a demolition permit, had announced that they would tear down the Senator and replace it with a parking garage. Vigils, appeals to the city, parades, phone calls, letters, and incredible round-the-clock coverage by radio and TV kept the Senator standing. An encouraging fusion of aesthetics with politics enabled the mayor to arrive at a unique plan whereby the Senator would be saved and municipal parking lots created across the street. Our collective imagination soared at the prospect of seeing the Senator's sixty rooms cleaned and polished once again and having this wonderful building used for public functions or become a center for preservation groups, a museum, or a model hotel.

This book is dedicated to the memory of my mother, Myrtle Bacharach Baer, a painter, sculptor, and designer of the thirties who helped develop the style; and to my grandchildren Jason, William, Catherine, and Jamila, in the hope that they will find the Art Deco District still intact when they are old enough to enjoy it.

It is a pleasure to be able to express my thanks and gratitude to the following for their help given to me in so many ways: John M. Allen; T.D. Allman; Valerie Batts, Ph.D.; Robert Bishop, Ph.D.; Andrew Capitman; John Capitman, Ph.D.; Thelma Chavin; Margaret Doyle; Joseph Z. Fleming; Andrea Freedman; Dorothy Gaiter; Marion Goldman; Thorne Grafton, AIA; Dahlia Greene; Christopher Heid; Richard Hoberman; Leonard L. Horowitz, IDSA; Michael Kinnerk; Marion Levien; Ernest Martin, Ph.D.; Cyril I. Nelson; David Nevel; Michael O'Connor; Mary Paget; David Pearlson; Evelyn Perlman; Denise Scott-Brown; Nicole Sultan; Fred Tasker.

CONTENTS

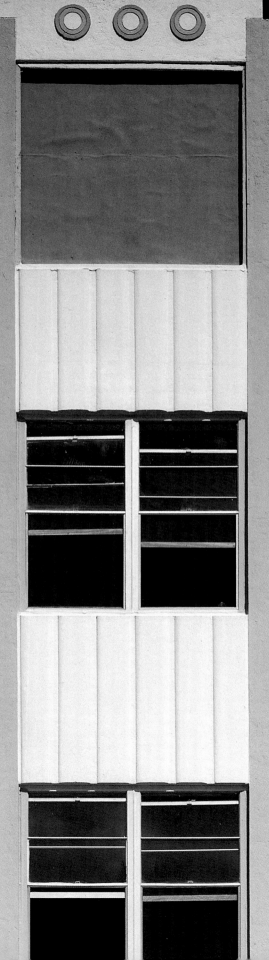

PREFACE

For the second time Miami Beach is hosting Art Deco Weekend, the annual celebration of the city's architectural treasure trove, without one of the historic district's most lustrous gems.

The 46-year-old Cardozo Hotel, with its jazz bands, "Deco Delights" desserts and wrap-around porch overlooking the Atlantic, is darkened. The lobby is empty, save for step ladders lying on the floor and a stack of carpet rolls in one corner.

—Dory Owens,
"Deco Owners' Rocky Road,"
Miami Herald, January 6, 1986

"Deco Delights" was the name of the famous sinful dessert made of chocolate fudge squares, vanilla ice cream, and whipped cream. Prepared behind the glass counter of the Cardozo Café, Deco Delights were featured in the period 1979 to 1983, now regarded as Camelot by the survivors of that time who are still working and living in the Art Deco District. My son Andrew, at the age of thirty, opened the café and took the concoction and adapted the name from the deck lunch counter at the Vineyard Haven Yacht Club in Massachusetts, where he had learned a lot about the good but simple life and where he also conceived a passion for "Vineyard Delights."

Now the Cardozo is open again; there are many good places to hang out and dine in the District, and Deco Delights has now achieved a broader meaning. The title of this book refers to the buildings themselves, and even more to the manifold pleasures of the District: the sound, fashion, life-style, art, joyful events, and world renown generated here.

PRESERVING THE BEAUTY AND JOY OF MIAMI BEACH ARCHITECTURE

When the sun comes up with the suddenness of a tropical dawn, it rises over the Atlantic Ocean, over the tankers and cruisers waiting on the horizon to enter the Port of Miami, and it shines brilliantly also on the nation's only Art Deco District.

On Ocean Drive luggage is set out on the hotel porches overlooking the sidewalk, as guests appear to wait for limousines to the first flights out from the airport. Pink linen cloths are placed on the tables for early morning breakfast, and joggers run along the beach, glancing up at the skyline of pastel-colored shapes rising above the fringe of palms. In the park a class of elderly exercisers stretches toward the cloudless sky. A photography crew and models in white cottons gather in the street preparing for still another shoot.

The sound of tennis balls on the Flamingo courts begins while a youthful stockbroker emerges from a green and pink Deco apartment house across from the tennis court and plucks a gardenia for his buttonhole from a flowering bush in the courtyard as he moves toward his Porsche convertible parked on the street.

Activity will continue late into the night, as new restaurants and refurbished theatres and discos and stores, which open at 10 P.M. for the night crowds, draw thousands of young people, dressed in costume, in office clothes, and in formal attire. As it had been in the heyday of the area, neon signs and illuminated coves and backlighted glass block glow once again, and shop windows displaying tempting Deco collectibles—posters, crystal vases, chrome cocktail shakers—lure the new species of collector, the Decophile, to browse and buy.

The Art Deco District, the country's latest "in" place—a place of infinite complexity and appeal—is at a point of decision.

One night in August 1987, Steven Brooke, the noted architectural photographer who took the splendid photographs for this book, stood before one hundred and fifty people gathered at the popular Deco restaurant, the Strand, to discuss the impending demolition of the Senator Hotel. "I am photographing the District for this book Barbara and I are doing," he said, putting his hand touchingly on my shoulder as I sat on the podium, "and I am hurrying to document it all—all these little buildings—because I don't know from day to day which will still be standing. And I want to tell you this: unless we make a great effort, what we will have in the end is simply this, the record we are making now, photographs, not buildings, not streetscapes."

Our meeting had come together to repel the unthinkable act of demolishing the Senator, L. Murray Dixon's 1939 spired and shining structure, which was built with the new elegance of modern architecture between the wars. It was an example of Deco architecture rather similar to other Deco landmarks in Amsterdam or London or Seattle, and yet it was different, a mixture of Deco styles concocted especially for Collins Avenue in Miami Beach. Whether or not the Senator will be saved is a question for the future. We have had these battles before—and lost! And we have all—public and preservationists—learned a great deal about the elusive, creative, and innocent brave new world of Miami Beach of almost half a century ago that gave birth to this unique environment.

When our publisher came down from New York with my good friend Robert Bishop, director of the Museum of American Folk Art in New York City, we, too, were innocent. We proposed a book that would be as straightforward and as charming as E. P. Dutton's *Painted Ladies*, which is all about San Francisco's resplendently painted Victorian houses. We were so proud of our newly repainted, restored buildings in the Art Deco District, and we wanted to put together a volume similar to *Painted Ladies*, which would show the Deco apartment buildings and hotels in all their recaptured crisp and colorful fantasy. Our earlier publication, *Portfolio*, produced with a National Endowment for the Arts grant in 1979 with photographs by David Kaminsky, and subsequently used as the photographic record for Laura Czerwinske's book, *Tropical Deco*, burst on the preservation world as something startlingly novel. It was as novel as the architecture itself in the thirties, but the color in the photographs we took to Washington seems so drab now that we are all so accustomed to the "Miami Vice" palette. Yet *Portfolio* thrilled conservationists in Washington, used to leaden skies and dour brick, and similarly at a meeting of the National Trust in San Francisco in 1979, our message was a revelation about twentieth-century architecture just waiting to be brought back to glowing life in every city.

In March, however, we were not prepared for an objective look at the District today. So many buildings still bright in our memories from the time when they had first been restored had since grown shabby, or had been boarded up, or were in the middle of wrenching restoration. Even Lummus Park was being dug up for what is to become a widened Ocean Drive. We were seeing real estate development and land speculation on every side. Properties were being land-banked (an expression new to us), just waiting for new investors to offer double and triple the purchase price; restaurants and nightclubs were changing ownership, sometimes losing their initial design éclat.

What follows is a reaction to some of the events of the summer of 1987—an attempt, supported by Steven's beautiful photographs, to reveal the Art Deco District as it was conceived by its handful of sophisticated architects: Henry Hohauser, Larry Dixon, Albert Anis, and their colleagues. Obviously, because we were looking more closely at the

buildings that seemed threatened, for we felt we were fighting for their continued existence, we were made even more aware of their unique contribution to that spectacular era. Far from being isolated, merely regional artists creating a poor-man's version of the dazzling skyscraper Deco of the big cities, Miami Beach architects were creating a brilliant sculptural addendum to the Deco story, for they were caught up in the wave of modernism, the love of twentieth-century industrial design. Their accomplishment is one that the many books and exhibits on Art Deco that appeared in the eighties have tended largely to ignore.

The Art Deco District has become, since we brought it back, that phenomenon of our time: an important "tourist destination." It is also a struggling neighborhood with a new demography, and a center for cultural events and entertainment. It is time to try to rethink its genesis, and its future.

Discovering the Deco Heritage

In the summer of 1987, Vyonne Geneve, then fifty-three, an artist-professor at the University of Perth, Western Australia, arrived in the Art Deco District, the most important destination on her travel grant. Ten thousand miles away she had poured over architectural magazines and syndicated newspaper stories, and when she left her Mexican-style ranch house and family, she knew that if she were to lead the movement to save the Art Deco movie houses and hotels in Australia's America's Cup Races city on the other side of the world, although she would travel though the United States, she would have to come to Miami Beach, the source of the contemporary Art Deco revival movement to see what was happening and to find out how to do it herself.

Professor Geneve, like so many of our visitors, came with insights about the style. She had become an expert on an Australian regional architect, William T. Leighton, who was responsible for many of the major Art Deco theatres in Sydney and Perth. From the atmospheric theatres that took their cue from the work of the American firm, Eberson and Eberson (designers of our own Gusman theatre), to the later suave modernistic theatres clad in black Vitrolite and chrome, which provided escape into Hollywood fantasy during the war, Leighton's development mirrors the path of Deco designers around the world. In his architect's journey from baroque excess and ornamentation to a stripping away to provide staid Australian streets with Moderne elegance, he was accomplishing just what Deco designers were achieving in the United States.

The Bentley Hotel at 5th Street and Ocean Drive, although one block short of the National District boundary on 6th Street, is the southern launching point. Built in 1939, and designed by John and Carlton Skinner, it is one of the few Ocean Drive hotels to incorporate stores on the first floor. Octagonal windows and a cut-corner entrance draw one around the corner. Restoration by Streamline Development enhances the horizontal banding and crisp line. The octagonal plaque with the fountain motif echoes the windows and announces the special Deco quality of Ocean Drive.

The Park Central Hotel, 630 Ocean Drive, 1937, is one of Henry Hohauser's best efforts, and it has the high ceilings and spaciousness of a true oceanfront resort. Seven stories tall, it is scaled with such simplicity that it seems smaller. Redeveloped by Tony Goldman, the Park Central and the neighboring Imperial will feature luxury restaurants and appointments. Etched glass, a deep porch shaded by a tin canopy, and gleaming terrazzo from the front steps through the vast lobby are features. Designer Leonard Horowitz, who originated the Deco Revival pastel palette, here used basic white spruced up by mauve and green verticals.

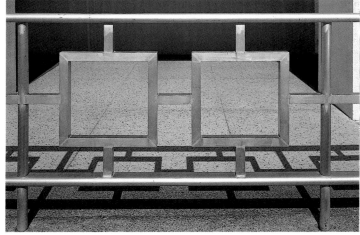

A detail of the handsome balustrade fronting the Park Central.

The Imperial at 650 Ocean Drive is a fine example of the accord with which in 1939 the master architects worked. Designed in 1939 by L. Murray Dixon two years later than the Park Central (its next-door neighbor), it shares the white, mauve, and green color scheme of the Park Central. Note the handsome floral plaques in the green vertical bands. As late as 1983 the Imperial and the 600 block were considered one of the worst crime spots on the Beach. MDPL members repainted the lobby themselves and redesigned the facade. Also, they held parties there during an election campaign to prove that the lights and music of preservation activities could really change the neigborhood.

What our Australian visitor discovered was an Art Deco world in full swing: even in steamy July thousands of young people partied at new nightclubs; political fights raged over a threatened demolition; real estate changed hands even as she watched; the leading newspaper, the *Miami Herald*, had just published an unprecedented seven-section Sunday article on the District; hundreds of artisans were busy painting, plastering, and roofing as buildings were restored before her eyes, and other buildings that she had seen illustrated in journals and travel supplements were standing boarded up and neglected. When Professor Geneve left Miami, however, she was inspired, not so much by the architecture, which she liked, as by the way it could be used as the foundation of a city's revival. A resort could be re-created in Perth by using the similar early twentieth-century, curvilinear, streamlined stucco buildings as the base on which to build. She also had a better understanding of the question scholars kept asking in Australia: how did the American Art Deco style come to Perth? She had watched Miamians struggling with that same question: how had Miami architects, located almost as far south as one could go, arrive at this urban, international style?

But Professor Geneve, rather than just answering art-historical questions, could now envision swimmers coming to the porch of Perth's Black Swan Hotel for afternoon drinks, faces flushed with sun and health, listening to thirties Big Band music, and being happily sated with the beauty of the river and the white buildings where their parents and grandparents had danced and reveled.

Today, it is hard for anyone, whether from Australia or just from Miami across Biscayne Bay, to realize that in 1976 the term *Art Deco* was barely known, and that the area, so vibrant today, was considered a disgrace to the city, because of its cheap neon lights, "funny-shaped" buildings, and the signs along Ocean Drive blaring "rooms $5 a week."

The Discovery Phase

In 1976, America was getting ready to observe its Bicentennial—the rediscovery of America's heritage—and the environmental, think-small, zero-growth ideology still prevailed. As a relative newcomer to Miami, surviving the stunning blow of my husband's death, I gravitated to the American Society of Interior Designers' (ASID) meetings for companionship, and there I found others who were not that happy about the new buildings, like the huge Omni, just beginning to be built along the bay. At a cocktail party Leonard Horowitz, a young designer,

and I decided to form a new association that would present alternative ideas about what designers might find valuable in Miami, a place of startling juvenescence to one like myself who had owned a whaling-captain's house on Martha's Vineyard off the coast of Massachusetts. We gathered together a group of five designers one June afternoon and founded the Miami Design Preservation League (MDPL), and we were determined to locate an area to express our views.

By December 1, 1976, we had discovered Art Deco, the design style that best expressed what was special about Miami. Leonard also knew something I didn't: that Art Deco already had vast numbers of admirers—people who were collecting in the field and who had visited the 1968 furniture show in New York City at the Finch School. We made our announcement in Design Row—already a wonderful enclave of wholesale showrooms in Miami, the center for the designers and architects who were furnishing high-rise apartment buildings all over Florida. In preparation for the meeting we sent out groups to scout the Miami area for a place to stage our struggle for heritage awareness and growth containment, and much like making an archaeological discovery of some ancient forgotten city, we came inevitably upon South Beach in Miami. Suddenly, my apartment on Venetian Island, hanging over Biscayne Bay, was filled with youthful artists and designers. Woody Vondracek, then a mechanic at Eastern Airlines, appeared with his first poster, a stark Deco tower. Four hundred designers showed up at the meeting and pledged to help re-create "Old Miami Beach" and to save the depressed population of elderly people who lived there. For the first time a Deco party was held in Miami. Slides of Deco hotels were flashed on the walls. Twenties clothes were modeled and jazz played. A contemporary blacksmith from Savannah showed slides; no one had realized that the modern design of the Deco period was also used on gates and railings. A preservationist came from Greenville, North Carolina, and we reeled with visions of street celebrations, like those celebrating old architecture in Greenville. But it was Leicester Hemingway, Ernest's kid brother, who summed up for us the heritage that was waiting there across the bay to be extolled and restored:

Architects were determined not to use any older styles like the Spanish...they didn't quite know where they were headed; but they wanted something modern, so they smoothed out all the Spanish things. They smoothed the balconies, they smoothed everything until you got the feeling that life was smooth. The buildings made you feel all clean and new and excited and happy to be there.

On a Sunday afternoon in January 1977, a group gathered on the the keystone steps of that replica of Christopher Columbus's house in Genoa, the Amsterdam Palace on Ocean Drive. We were headed by the late Carl Weinhardt, Jr., the director of Viscaya and an ardent Art Deco expert, and by Frederick Bland, a young architect, now a senior partner in a New York firm, and we divided into teams and walked the incipient district for the first time, noting the style and scope of the little apartment houses and hotels. When we regrouped, Carl gathered our notes and maps and made the pronouncement we longed to hear: "The area is definitely Deco."

We MDPL members began to attend city meetings in the old city hall, left vacant when the city administration moved to the new city hall in 1978. The old city hall had reopened after restoration last year. We were a new element to appear at Beach meetings, a lobbyist group of distinguished citizens—designers, museum directors, editors. In 1977 we obtained our first grant: $10,000 from the City Planning Department to conduct a survey and plan for preservation in Miami Beach.

The Identification Phase

How the district became the District, the inspiration for cities from Perth to Philadelphia, the magnet for sentimental journeys and historic safaris, is a tale of many unsung volunteers and long hours spent photographing and cataloguing.

In 1978, we were able to give the city the report that became the basis for subsequent planning, and only a year later we nominated and won the designation of the area to the National Register of Historic Places. We had identified over 1,200 buildings on Miami Beach, from 1st Street to 24th, as "historic," and we began to assemble them into stylistic categories, with most being either Art Deco or Spanish/Mediterranean. We went on to identify various areas of the Beach and to choose one in particular, roughly the present National District, as the center for historic buildings. Seldom had so many buildings been classified for preservation purposes. Certainly, this was a first close look at whole blocks of twentieth-century buildings. It was startling to discover that there were so many buildings that expressed one style. On Saturday mornings teams would go out and return to find the press waiting to hear what had been found. We were experiencing the excitement of an archaeological dig.

The District and its Boundaries

Twenty blocks, a square mile, of Miami Beach that are listed on the National Register of Historic Places were selected as the most intensively Deco area remaining of a much larger Deco-inspired Beach and even of a greater Miami. The boundaries were selected by a committee led by a state architectural historian, a county historian, three student interns, the Miami Beach City Planner, and myself. We set these boundaries with visions of great entrances, buffer zones, promenades, and such natural boundaries as Dade Canal. The result can be found today in the phone book, AAA maps, tourist documents, and so forth.

It is bounded on the south by the city's new venture called South Pointe, a proposed development of highrises intended for the very rich and yuppies. South Pointe has been in process for all the years the District has been developing. It already closes off the streets to the south with an urban wall, a massive apartment tower. This new building broods over the new waterfront park that edges South Beach. All this fronts Florida's most dramatic entry from the Atlantic Ocean called Government Cut, whence the great ocean liners come into the Port of Miami, along with sailing ships, "Cigarettes," and other speedboats, hulking rusted tankers, and cargo ships from all over the world.

On the east, there is the beach, the four-year-old, $72-million-dollar beach, fringed from 5th to 15th streets by the coconut palms that the first settler, Henry Lum, planted in expectation of making a fortune. From the beach appears a skyline that emerged from three decades of neglect to form now a dainty silhouette of pastel castles, unlike any shoreline in the world. On the west the District stops one alley shy of Alton Road, planned for big commerce. Beyond Alton are the high-rise condominiums of West Avenue, cutting off from the east the view of Biscayne Bay near which they stand, and for the people who live on the islands to the west the view of the ocean once visible from Venetian Island. These buildings too are changing, for gradually their harsh contours are being softened by Deco pinks and greens, and their demography is becoming more youthful. Younger families are now moving in to go to work right across the bay in the new Miami of multinational international commerce, to the towering offices of granite and glass, glowing at night with the Beach's colors, washes of Miami man-made illumination.

To the north, finally, there is the supersize Convention Center. The new section being built is

The Waldorf Towers, 860 Ocean Drive, designed by Albert Anis in 1937, sweeps around the corner, its streamlining enhanced by the continuous "eyebrows," or *brise soleil*. Incredibly, its wonderful tower, one of the most delightful sights on Ocean Drive, was considered unsafe and ordered torn down by the City in the early 1980s. Fortunately, it was rebuilt by developer Gerry Sanchez in 1985 as a first gesture of respectful preservation. At night a line of blue neon encircles the tower and glows in the signage. Waldorf suites, developed by Don Maginley, encourage TV and other media to work and shoot from the Waldorf, and its downstairs bar is the scene for jazz buffs.

One of Henry Hohauser's first hotels was the little Colony, built in 1935 at 736 Ocean Drive. The facade was a victim of inappropriate brick veneering, but the lobby remains one of the District's prizes with its fireplace faced with green Vitrolite and a Diego Rivera–like mural by Ramon Chatov.

The photograph of the lobby of the Waldorf Towers on the opposite page shows the handsome terrazzo floor, the use of glass block under the window, and the splendid Deco lighting fixtures in the recessed ceiling, which are reflected in the mirror over the fireplace of tinted scagliola. The photographs on this page illustrate the molded ceiling and terrazzo in greater detail.

Here are two more terrazzo patterns from the District. Frequently designed by the 85 versatile architects themselves, terrazzo is now enjoying a revival. It is composed of stone chips set in mortar and polished when dry. The Deco District is probably the world's richest source of this type of flooring. In England and elsewhere theatres used linoleum inlays to obtain the same effect.

Pehaps the most highly regarded gourmet restaurant on Ocean Drive is the Café des Artes, owned by interior designer/preservationist Sandra Cook. It is located on the ground floor of the Locust, built in 1926, which is Venetian Gothic/Mediterranean Revival in style. Residents of the converted apartments obtain a stunning ocean view through the third-floor arched windows. The meticulous details of tiled floors, planting, and paintings make the Locust a true example of fantasy design.

over the famous patch of greensward that the nation looked at in the summer of 1972, when the Republican Convention was fought out on its grass. Beyond that to the north from Indian Creek to Biscayne Bay is an exclusive and beautiful residential neighborhood, designed in the twenties and thirties by the same architects who designed the buildings of the District. It is filled with an untapped textbook of residential design ideas, from Mayan friezes and temple gates culled from the early part of the century's infatuation with archaeology to stellar examples of Corbusier-like streamlined houses, secure behind curving concrete walls and glass blocks. Here sprinklers softly water the flowers and clipped grass in a silence remote from the excitement of the District only a few blocks away.

The story of the identification phase is not clear until one realizes how close the call was. Ocean Drive and all that lay behind it to the west was slated to be Phase 11 of a plan to revive the Beach by repeating the concrete canyons of the north section of the city.

This plan was the background for the city's refusal to embrace the District concept of a preserved Art Deco resort. Over the years visitors would exclaim, "Are they crazy? Can't they see what you have here!" But the political pattern had been set. The land, the site, were too valuable for the small buildings. The formula for development was to continue despite the District's acclaim. Summer 1987 provided the opportunity they had awaited for so long. Harmony, compromise with the preservationists, and lip service to the District had paved the way for demolition and for building new large towers again.

The first decisive victory against the prodevelopment forces was the listing on the National Register in 1979. Another fact that is hard to believe now, not even ten years later, is that the Register listing was vehemently opposed by City Hall. After a long bitter public battle that reached the architectural press and Paul Goldberger in *The New York Times*, the state's Architectural Board of Review voted unanimously in February 1979 in favor of the District. Our delegation of ten had journeyed to the University of Florida at Gainesville for this hearing along with the opposition force consisting of the City Manager and the Chamber of Commerce. We joined a packed hall of architectural students and the press giving wild, moving cheers. It had not been clear whether or not the ten distinguished scholars on the Review Panel would give in to the pressure on them to turn down the nomination.

The news went around the world. Art Deco architecture had become official. Approved! The decision signified that a new category of American architecture was officially part of our heritage. The Empire State Building, Hoover Dam, the Paramount Theatre in Oakland, California, the Board of Trade on LaSalle Street in Chicago—all could now take their places with Gettysburg, Monticello, Mount Vernon, the Alamo, which are listed among America's historic places. The listing also meant that a new hunt had begun to find and identify obscure and often endangered buildings, warehouses, garages and gas stations, commercial strips, neighborhood movie theatres, bridge decorations and public lighting, hotels, homes—the list was long. A new galaxy had been added to the preservation constellation. These buildings were now eligible for tax benefits.

The Design Team—A Common Stylistic Quest

At the start of our revival effort, we tended to be apologetic about District buildings individually. Joy Moos, the Miami gallery owner, and I led a group of MDPL leaders to New York in 1980 to form an international Art Deco organization. Appropriately, Knoll International, one of the great firms in modern furniture design, threw a lavish party, and the guest list was stellar—the architects who supported us, the design press, and Art Deco dealers like Lillian Nassau (who later that year was to be honored by the City of New York for her contribution in the field of Art Nouveau). I remember my feeling of humility addressing this group on behalf of the District—our Deco, I said, is different. You in New York with the splendor of your murals, and sculpture and pinnacles of beauty, must realize that we are talking about an altogether different Deco—plainer, made from cheaper materials, which takes its strength from the impact of there being so many buildings created in the same style.

The Register nomination, the experts who came to pronounce the importance of the District, all said the same thing. If you took any single building in the district and compared it to the Chrysler Building in New York, it would be a sad comparison.

Often quoted was a statement in *Art in America* by John Perreault. He asked in 1981: "Are any of these buildings masterpieces? Probably not. Yet the Art Deco District in its entirety is a kind of architectural masterpiece...an unparalleled streetscape that not only reflects a particular time, climate and economy, but also offers lessons to those seriously committed to a more human urban environment."

But as the decade of discovery became the decade of revival restoration, a new appreciation for the buildings was born from the fact of our living in them, photographing them, promoting and restoring them.

Looking south from the Colony, we are impressed by an extraordinary example of Ocean Drive as "roadside architecture" with signage that beckons us through design and by the cubist shapes of the closely packed buildings. ▶

The Breakwater, at 940 Ocean Drive, and the Edison, at 1060, are linked by a wonderful pool, used by both hotels, that has a Neptune mosaic on its bottom. Both hotels are owned by Gerry Sanchez's Polonia Corporation, but they are quite opposite in style. The Breakwater, 1939, by Anton Skislewicz, like his Plymouth Hotel on 21st Street, is a smooth soaring expression of New York World's Fair modernism. Its double-faced signage mounting a concrete tower, and suggestive of Mayan design, is its chief feature. The roof deck and horizontal racing stripes have the flat geometry of a De Stijl painting. Les Beilinson, AIA, is responsible for the restoration architecture for both the Breakwater and Edison.

By 1985, Katharine Maddox, News Editor of *Vogue*, in writing an article about Miami as being one of seven great cities of the United States, again put the emphasis on the entirety of the District, but at an even more positive level:

> I was excited to bursting by what I found a few blocks to the south of the Fontainebleau. Of course I'd heard about the fabulous Art Deco zone in lower Miami Beach, seen plenty of photos. Still; I was totally unprepared for its extent, its quality, its magic. For sheer invention, Deco was one of America's most amazing periods, and the architectural pleasures of *a common stylistic quest* reveal themselves in detail after detail in the hundreds of buildings that make up one of our greatest environments, so colorful like sinking into cotton candy.

And the following statement was made in the September 1977 issue of *Eastern Review,* illustrated with striking photographs by Michael O'Connor:

> The Deco District in Miami Beach is the largest in the world and its various buildings explore the range of stylistic possibilities. Despite each building's idiosyncrasies there remains a thematic harmony based on Art Deco's central tenets; each component of an Art Deco neighborhood or building must contribute to the total effect...the buildings in Miami Beach testify to their creators' vision of perfect aesthetic accord.

What has been almost entirely ignored is a rare and unusual banding together of a small group of artists, craftsmen, engineers, and construction firms, under the leadership of a handful of architects, carrying out the development of an unplanned city in the very latest and most visionary style. The style was so advanced that only today is the design world catching up to its accomplishment. Today, such a project with so many buildings might never happen; it would get lost in the bureaucratic maze of planners, auditors, and lawyers.

Perhaps the stigma of regionalism is the cause for undervaluing the work of the architects. In the thirties, one of the worst things one could say about an artist was that he was a "regionalist." Grant Wood and Thomas Hart Benton were so labeled. It meant that they were too realistic in their painting, too reactionary about abstraction, and tended to be too nationalistic about modernism in general. They would never end up in The Museum of Modern Art. Of course, this judgment has been reversed over the decades, and today there is no lack of regard for this school of American painting. The same thing is not true, however, for regional *architects*. What makes it more difficult to seek official regard for what they achieved is that frequently they were not recognized by their peers when they lived. In Miami, this denigration still goes on. Older architects who remember Hohauser, for example, tend to shrug off his accomplishment. "Oh, I know what he was doing: he was just a good businessman, selling resort architecture. Not a real architect," said one pillar of the American Institute of Architects (AIA) more than once. The architects who created the concrete canyons, the masses of high rises on Venetian Causeway, continue to be the heroes. The adulation of world-famous architects like Philip Johnson and Robert Venturi for the District leaves them unmoved. They are still listening to their professors from the fifties who tended to pass over Deco architecture. The 1988 summer exhibtion on Miami architecture at the Bass Museum is helping the architectural fraternity to reexamine outmoded positions.

The basic core of thirties architects, says Paul Silverthorne, interior designer and muralist for the group, included L. Murray Dixon, Henry Hohauser, Albert Anis, Roy France, Russell Pancoast, Igor Polevitsky, Anton Skislewicz, and others.

They used a kind of hands-on approach, for many AIA architects, like Frank Lloyd Wright, had degrees in engineering, but not in architecture. They were fascinated by the new materials being used and experimented with them in combination with local concrete and coral stone, and studied the architects' manuals on such subjects as the light diffusion and insulation properties of glass block. The architects had great respect for the artists on the team, and in fact, some of the artists were also architects—such as Robert Swartburg, who had an impressive educational background in the field.

Among the others in the group was Herman Glasser, known as "the glass king." His son, Leonard (a leader in MDPL before his death in 1980), also became a major architect in the District, designing apartment buildings after the war that maintained the scale and spirit of the District. Herman Glasser's etched windows and panels were to be seen everywhere: in the windows of the Senator, Tiffany, and Breakwater hotels, in the lobby of the French Casino, and over the doors of the New Yorker. They were the major applied decoration used by the architects to convey the sense of a particular place—tropical Florida.

Through the architects' offices (Hohauser's was located over a streamlined theatre on 41st Street, Commissioner Ben Grenald remembers) came plasterers and painters ready for any challenge, upholsterers, lighting engineers, and sign makers. Lawrence Dixon, Jr., stresses today that the architects, like the industrial designers they had known in New York, were holistic in their approach to the design problem. They designed carpeting, terrazo patterns, lighting, and built-in custom cabinets like Dixon's cigarette drawers in the Hotel Victor, which swing open at the touch of a finger.

"Lobbies were planned to take advantage of the seashore sites," Earl LaPan told me when I first went to his studio in Dania in 1979. "It was a new thing then to bring the indoors out and the outdoors in. Gardens, front lawns and porches, the beach across the street, were living rooms. The lobbies and dining rooms and the murals continued the sense of being outdoors—the tropical sense."

"The architects I rubbed elbows with," says Paul Silverthorne, now seventy-six, "worked very hard. Contrary to what some critics say, they were much more than good salesmen. They were the ones who had the new ideas and carried them out."

Dixon and Hohauser—Preeminent

L. Murray Dixon, Jr., AIA, was a year old when his father came to the Beach in 1928. They came from New York where Dixon, Sr., a graduate of the Georgia Institute of Technology, had worked with one of the most important architectural firms of the times: Schultze and Weaver, designers of the Biltmore Hotel in Coral Gables and New York's Waldorf-Astoria Hotel (recently restored to its Art Deco brilliance, as advertising states, at a cost of $110 million). Dixon had been on his way back to Atlanta in 1933, during a lull in building, when he sat next to a Mr. Schultze on the train. Out of this chance encounter came Dixon's years in New York. His desk at the firm was next to that of Edward Durrell Stone, who was to become a major modern architect, and the architect for The Museum of Modern Art in New York City, when it opened in its own building on West 53rd Street in 1939.

Dixon, Jr., grew up being carried on his father's shoulders to the sites of the new buildings going up, riding the construction elevators, playing in the storefront studio on Euclid Avenue. "I learned the smells and sounds of architecture early on," he says. The office with its catwalk second floor, like the deck of an ocean-going ship's boiler room, for draftsmen, and long drafting tables hinged to the wall for spreading out blueprints, had a little conference room behind a curving wall of glass block. Here the design team that worked on the District frequently gathered, for they were all good friends. "There was too much work in the latter part of the thirties for unfriendly competition," says Dixon's son.

Before he left Miami, eighteen years later, Dixon,

Sr., was to report to the AIA that he had designed 40 hotels, 87 apartment houses, 229 residences, 2 housing developments, 33 store buildings, and 31 alterations (among them, changes on Lincoln Road from the Mediterranean style to Art Deco), as well as the impressive Miami Post Office and Customs buildings (with other architects). When he first came to Miami Beach, Dixon worked with architect George Fink, cousin to a Coral Gables developer and a designer of many Spanish residences there. Fink was also a mayor of Miami Beach and an influence on the Beach's Spanish-style buildings.

Later, Dixon was to serve on the Board of the National Council of Architectural Registry. His son recounts his father's fall from a fourth-floor building site and how he lay recovering in bed for months and reading "baskets of books" his mother would bring from the library—one way he kept in touch with current trends.

Grace Hohauser, whose husband, Henry, came to Miami in 1932 at the age of thirty-seven with a sophisticated architectural background, stated that *he* was the person who brought modernism to the Beach. There is every reason to believe she is right, and that he was the great influencer of the able architects who took up the cause, Dixon in particular. Hohauser's most publicized work in the District seems to have been the particular victim of a thoughtless city administration. A current commissioner first brought Hohauser as a master architect to world attention by destroying the New Yorker Hotel, a streamlined hotel with Mayan decoration, considered to be of exceptional distinction.

Then the city marked the smaller Neron Hotel (also designed by Hohauser) for demolition in order to build the huge new Justice Center on Washington Avenue. This new building meant the loss of an entire square block of District apartment houses. An attempt was at least made to incorporate the Neron facade in the new building, but that idea, acceptable to the architects, a city-sponsored firm, was scotched so that the new police headquarters could sweep around a curve where the Neron had been, in a manner supposedly Deco in style.

A graduate of Pratt Institute in Brooklyn, Hohauser worked in the large New York office of a cousin, William Hohauser, and became an ardent follower of the modern movement. He was stimulated, for example, by the opening in 1929 of The Museum of Modern Art at its first site and attended the first exhibit of paintings by Cézanne, Seurat, Gauguin, and van Gogh. The 42nd Street skyscrapers were built while Hohauser was still in New York—for example, the Chanin building by Sloane and

The Edison is *not* some 1920s holdover of south Florida's Mediterranean style, but a Hohauser design of 1935, the same year he designed the curvaceous Colony down the street. The Edison was the first large-scale restoration to explore the Mediterranean Revival style. Although it had the advantage of a fine location and a pool, developers and preservationists alike had overlooked the Edison because it was not true Deco. Now it houses the Beach's loudest and perhaps wildest restaurant, the Tropics, carried out in Memphis-style design—a strange and rather exhilarating mixture of Spanish columns and vivid splatters of color. The charm of the hotel's porches, gazebo, and pool serve the District well on such occasions as a vast gathering of Latin American clergy and supporters at the Pope's 1987 visit to Miami. The Edison restoration used all the great Hohauser details: the three-story spiraled column topped by an arch, the roof line with dentils, and the arcaded porch.

The Victor, 1144 Ocean Drive, by L. Murray Dixon, 1937, has a signage pylon thrusting up to cubistic forms at the top. The building projects over a deep porch. Empty since 1984 when the Royale group purchased it, large-scale alterations have been approved by the city's Design Review Board. Note the moongate in the wall in the foreground.

The Leslie, 1244 Ocean Drive, by Albert Anis, 1937, is an example of fine classic Deco, and it contrasts well with the exuberance of the Carlyle next door.

This view of Ocean Drive to the north shows how the Leslie, the Carlyle, and the Cardozo are integrated. In the foreground is one of three "oases" designed by the late Andres Fabregas. It is an MDPL project—the first Deco street furniture: slatted benches, pink paving, and circular "Saturn" lamps in the newly widened Lumus Park. The future for these miniparks is clouded.

The Carlyle, 1250 Ocean Drive, by Kiehnel and Elliott, 1941, with its striking verticle piers and horizontal lines emphasized by the sunshades rounding the corners.

The Cardozo, 1300 Ocean Drive, by Henry Hohauser, 1939, a masterpiece of streamlining severly altered by the Royale Corporation and still not completed.

The Clevelander, 1020 Ocean Drive, by Albert Anis, 1937, is being carefully restored by the Kay family. A 1950s pool kiosk has been made consonant with the period by the addition of a handsome, glass-block outdoor bar.

The Cavalier, 1320 Ocean Drive, by Roy F. France, 1936, is noted for the incised ornamentation and the smart lettering of its name at the top center of the facade. Leased by Don McGinley, the Cavalier is the center of a new preservation spin-off industry—media production.

Robertson. The friezes of flowers and geese, set in onto the facade gave the building an illusion of stepping back into a zoomorphic study. Abstracted plant forms had an Egyptian or Mayan primitive quality. Later, Hohauser was to incorporate these friezes, as were the others on the team, into decorations for the Miami Beach buildings. Also on 42nd Street he could study the fabulous Chrysler Building, with its tower and spire, its marquetry elevator doors and cabs, and its patterned floors extending to the street. The Chrysler was a major event in the growing modern movement across the country. It was part of Hohauser's intellectual baggage when he arrived in Miami in the years of mid-career when creative output often begins. Hohauser was also stirred by and worked for the fairs of the period, particularly the Chicago Century of Progress Exposition in 1933.

Mrs. Hohauser said that the people who supported her husband were not the local people, "who were still involved with Spanish architecture." His clients tended to be the affluent Jewish bankers and realtors with whom he had been associated in New York, and who were part of the booming post-Depression resort scene in the Catskills.

For Albert Anis the last years of the thirties decade were pivotal. In 1939, he was to contribute importantly to the lineup of the taller beachfront hotels along Collins Avenue, the streamlined Bancroft and Poinciana (the Poinciana was demolished in 1988). In 1937, he had designed what is, perhaps, Ocean Drive's most evocative hotel, the Waldorf Towers. Here the wraparound "eyebrow" ledges and horizontality speak of the modern movement, while the prominent lighthouse tower is a powerful reminder that this is indeed architecture for the seashore. Jutting out from the corner of the building, the nonfunctional tower with its encircling band of blue neon is an apt symbol of Anis's capacity for fantasy. In 1981, in a wave of destructive activity, the city's Unsafe Structures Board had the tower removed in an unannounced strike. But when he purchased the hotel in 1984, Gerry Sanchez fortunately rebuilt it.

By 1940, Anis was designing—with perhaps the greatest flair for unrestrained flamboyancy and fantasy of any of the group—the Berkeley Shore at Collins and 16th. A decorative central column dominates the arcade, rising from two rows of window wall to a spire supported by semicircular steps. Anis, as if to subdue the forward thrust of this vision, attaches to the flanking geometric planes on each side of the center column large cast plaques of early Deco design decorated with a stylized leaf motif. This interesting building, which was illustrated

in *The Wall Street Journal* as summarizing the District architecture, is slated for demolition.

Also in 1940, Anis responded to Hohauser's Governor Hotel of 1939, directly across the street, by designing the Tyler Hotel with its streamlined corner and large projecting fin. The Tyler has been well restored by David Pearlson, and it now houses the charming Heritage Café.

Another important member of the design group was Robert Swartburg, often called the "architect's architect" by his peers. This referred to some degree to his rigorous education and his love of classical design. Recognized by the AIA, as most of the group were not, he delivered a much-quoted speech when he was awarded an architectural prize as a student at the University of Florida at Gainesville. After Columbia University, Swartburg had gone into practice by himself in New York and maintained his own office through the years. He was to leave his signature on many public buildings in Miami after World War II: the Convention Center and the conversion of the library into the Bass Museum. He was chosen as one of three architects to work on Miami's giant Civic Center and was responsible for the Justice Wing, the Penitentiary, and the Circuit Court—Beaux Arts designs with a touch of stripped Deco. But the spirit of adventure set free in the thirties caused him in 1947 to design the most "outrageous" tower of them all, the Aztec-headdress fins for the Delano.

Nationally Known Architects

The team was pleased when some of the big architects from New York or Philadelphia came to town, such as the famous Thomas Lamb of Shreve, Lamb and Harmon, noted for his theatres throughout the country; or when Kiehnel and Elliott came from Pittsburgh. Richard Kiehnel, born in Germany, had studied at the University of Breslau and then gone on to the Ecole Nationale des Beaux Arts in Paris. In 1917, he designed El Jardin, one of Miami's most revered residences in the Mediterranean style, now a private school. Commissioned by a Pittsburgh steel magnate, El Jardin breaks away from traditional neoclassical and Beaux Arts residential architecture to become the "earliest-known, full-fledged Mediterranean Revival work in Miami."

In 1922, Kiehnel designed one of Miami's secret delights, the Scottish Rites Temple, pure Aztec with pyramid setbacks, and great fierce stone eagles gripping the corners of the building. In 1925, Kiehnel and Elliott were responsible for another Miami landmark, the Coconut Grove Theatre, now the

Players State Theatre. After a hiatus Kiehnel was called back to design the Carlyle Hotel. Inserting the streamlined building into the row on Ocean Drive between the Leslie and the Cardozo, Kiehnel reiterated the horizontal lines of the others just as if he had been an old member of the team. Although the side facing the Cardozo was quite plain, the southern side, separated from the Leslie by a small courtyard, rippled with receding curving walls that became an architectural trademark of the period.

Architecture of the Thirties at Miami Beach: A Chronology of Important Structures from 1930 to 1940 with the Name of the Architect

1930

Bass Museum (originally a library)—Russell T. Pancoast
The Shorecrest—Kiehnel and Elliott
Amsterdam Palace—Henry La Pointe

1931

Hotel Shelley—Henry J. Maloney

1934

The Alamac Hotel (restored as apartments in 1987)—V. H. Nellenbogen
The Clinton Hotel—Charles Neidler
The Paddock (originally a bar; best known as the pastel-colored Friedman's Bakery; now the Watergun clothing store)—E. L. Robertson
Hotel Franklin—V. H. Nellenbogen
Colony Theatre—R. A. Benjamin
The Lafayette—Henry J. Maloney
The Strand Restaurant (originally The Famous)—E. L. Robertson
Santa Barbara Apartments—Russell T. Pancoast

1935

The An-Nell Hotel—Henry Hohauser
Barclay Plaza Hotel—Kiehnel and Elliott
The Colony Hotel—Henry Hohauser
The Edwards Hotel—Henry J. Maloney
The Edison Hotel—Henry Hohauser
Lincoln Cinema—Robert E. Collins and Thomas Lamb
The Netherlands Hotel—E. L. Robertson
The Primrose Hotel—V. H. Nellenbogen
The Savoy Plaza Hotel—V. H. Nellenbogen

The 30s Promenade (originally S. H. Kress Co.)—T. Hunter Robertson

1936

The Astor Hotel—T. Hunter Robertson
The Beach Plaza Hotel—L. Murray Dixon
The Beacon Hotel—Henry O. Nelson
The Cavalier Hotel—Roy F. France
The Collins Plaza Hotel—Henry Hohauser
Coronet Apartments—Henry Hohauser
The Davis Hotel—Henry Hohauser
The Fairmount Hotel—L. Murray Dixon
The Kenmore Hotel—Anton Skislewicz
Ida M. Fisher Junior High School—August Geiger
Lincoln Road Office Building—Robert E. Collins
The Park Vendome—Henry Hohauser
The Peter Miller Hotel—Henry Hohauser
The Sassoon Hotel (originally Dempsey's Vanderbilt)—Henry Hohauser
The Taft Hotel—Henry Hohauser
The Tides Hotel—L. Murray Dixon

1937

Burdine's Department Store—Robert Law Weed
The Clevelander Hotel—Albert Anis
The Leslie Hotel—Albert Anis
The Main Post Office—Howard L. Cheney
The Lincoln Center Hotel—Igor B. Polevitsky
Twins Apartments—L. Murray Dixon
The Victor Hotel—L. Murray Dixon
The Waldorf Towers Hotel—Albert Anis

1938

The Adams Hotel—L. Murray Dixon
Cameo Theatre—Robert E. Collins
The Essex House Hotel—Henry Hohauser
The Flamingo Plaza Hotel—L. Murray Dixon
The Park Central Hotel—Henry Hohauser
The Shepley Hotel—L. Murray Dixon

1939

The Albion Hotel—Igor B. Polevitsky
The Bancroft Hotel—Albert Anis
The Bentley Hotel—John and Coulton Skinner
The Breakwater Hotel—Anton Skislewicz
The Cardozo Hotel—Henry Hohauser
The Commodore Hotel—Henry Hohauser
The Collins Park Hotel—Henry Hohauser
The Century Hotel—Henry Hohauser
The Dorchester Hotel—Frank Wyatt Wood

Here are two stylish gems at the northern end of Ocean Drive: the Crescent (left) at 1420, designed by Henry Hohauser in 1932, and the McAlpin, designed by L. Murray Dixon in 1940. At the time of this book's going to press the Crescent had just been transformed from a 43-room hotel into 22 apartments, including two-story penthouse units. Developer Jack Bergman of New York selected Les Beilinson, AIA, to redesign both the Crescent and the McAlpin. A detail photograph of the Crescent on the back of this book highlights the handsomeness of the new and unusual color scheme.

COLLINS AVENUE

The Tiffany Hotel, the southernmost of L. Murray Dixon's corner hotels, was built at 801 Collins Avenue with an imposing metal spire and faceted windows. Opened in 1939.

The Franklin Hotel, 860 Collins, was selected for a 1978 feature in *American Heritage* because it appeared conservative and so was more palatable to readers unused to Deco. It is a true transitional building designed in 1934 by V. H. Nellenbogen.

The Sherbrooke Cooperative apartment house at 901 Collins, designed by MacKay & Gibbs in 1947.

At 960 Collins, the little Troy Hotel designed by Albert Anis in 1941, has been delightfully remodeled. Note the four narrow openings in the parapet that frame the sky—a lovely touch!

The Fairmont, 1000 Collins, a vision in pink, yellow, and green designed by L. Murray Dixon in 1939 now offers The Fairmont Café and Bar, a very stylish garden restaurant designed by Les Beilinson, AIA, for Pieter Bakker.

One of Hohauser's best designs, the Essex House of 1938, at 1001 Collins, has been painted to bring out its Nautical Moderne quality. It is a corner building like the Senator. The Collins Avenue view shows the porthole windows. A new owner, Patricia Murphy, a Newport, R.I., innkepper, assures the future for this hostelry.

The Greystone Hotel—Henry Hohauser
The Governor Hotel—Henry Hohauser
The Imperial Hotel—L. Murray Dixon
The Kent Hotel—L. Murray Dixon
The Marlin Hotel—L. Murray Dixon
The Palmer House Hotel—L. Murray Dixon
The Poinciana Hotel (demolished 1988)—Albert Anis
The Royal Palm Hotel—Donald G. Smith
The Sands Hotel—Roy F. France
The St. Moritz Hotel—Roy F. France
The Senator Hotel—L. Murray Dixon
The Tiffany Hotel—L. Murray Dixon
The Tudor Hotel—L. Murray Dixon
The Winter Haven Hotel—Albert Anis

1940

The Abbey Hotel—Albert Anis
The Barnett Building—Albert Anis
The National Hotel—Roy F. France
The Neron (demolished 1982)—Henry Hohauser
The New Yorker Hotel (demolished 1980)—Henry Hohauser
The Plymouth Hotel—Anton Skislewicz
The Raleigh Hotel—L. Murray Dixon
The Ritz Plaza Hotel—L. Murray Dixon
The Tyler Hotel—Albert Anis
The China Club (formerly Ovo; originally Hoffman's Cafeteria)—Henry Hohauser

The Art Deco Revival—An Amazing Comeback

Art Deco as a design style is a twentieth-century phenomenon. Its roots were firmly planted at the turn of the century, and it reached its height during the interwar period: between 1920 and 1941. It was a reaction to the revolutions of our time—industrialization, invention, communication, and changes in society—the liberation of women, for example. It was pervasive, sweeping, democratic, and yet also elitist. It was both a dime-store style, when even that mode of retailing was new, and a New York style seen at the most exclusive shops on Fifth Avenue. It was the style of the great modern skyscrapers in cities across the country, yet it was also the style of the gas stations, diners, and motels that developed from the surge of Americans traveling by car.

In Miami Beach, Deco came to a climax in the last years of the thirties but it was already on the way in the mid-twenties, particularly with the development of fantasy buildings that had their genesis in Hollywood. In Miami Beach, as across the U.S., Art Deco meant a definite break with the past—with the galleried, wooden resort-style hotel and with the

large resorts like the Biltmore and the Roney Plaza in the Spanish/Mediterranean style.

It was a new style to accompany new tastes: Big Band and jazz in music, new streamlined trains bringing visitors down to Florida, sumptuous Cartier "mystery clocks" and jewelry being sold on Lincoln Road at stores sporting new, Moderne facades erected over the Spanish fronts similar to those on Worth Avenue in Palm Beach.

Then, suddenly, at Miami Beach and around the country, with the coming of World War II, it was all over. And after the war there were other new styles, basically developments of the International Style, and the work of the earlier architects and designers was forgotten. The thirties style was considered tacky, in bad taste, and old fashioned. There followed almost four decades of completely ignoring Art Deco—in Miami and all over the country. The fabulous Chrysler Building deteriorated in New York. The Union Terminal in Cincinnati, so busy during the war, was abandoned.

So how did Art Deco become reborn? How, after nearly three decades of silence, after three decades in the college design schools of students being taught to disregard all that "bad stuff" of the thirties, how did the whole picture change? Art Deco came back even more strongly than it had been in the days it was being created, when designers were going in numerous directions looking for ways to break from the past.

Post-Modernism

Perhaps the Deco Revival story began with the dissatisfaction among architects with modern architecture and its response to social problems. Some critics say that the official date of the "death of modern architecture" was the implosion of Pruitt-Igoe, an award-winning housing development in St. Louis. Pruitt-Igoe had been abandoned by its tenants because its impersonal conditions fostered crime. The Post-Modern movement in architecture tried through historical allusions and human-scale projects to bring about a new way of looking at the American past: the smooth curves, the nautical pipe railings, porthole windows, and glass block were favorite trademarks of this school of architecture.

Post-Modernists took up the cause of Art Deco Revival from the first. Robert Venturi and Denise Scott-Brown were the most vocal in supporting Art Deco at the Beach when it was still a term one avoided using in city-planning studies. When the world-famous Venturi, Rauch, and Scott-Brown architectural firm won the commission to plan a new Washington Avenue, they were bold enough to refer to it as the Deco Main Street. They were never asked to do another plan for the city. But their interest in Miami Beach Art Deco was shared by other Post-Modernists: Philip Johnson, Stanley Tigerman of Chicago, and Hugh Hardy of New York, then at work on the Willard Hotel in Washington, D.C. It became the cause of these architects' interest, a favorite subject of the architectural journals. As Post-Modernism became more acceptable so did the Art Deco Revival.

The Comeback

In 1981, Leonard Horowitz and I spent three months traveling 10,000 miles around the U.S. in my Chevette (like crossing the Atlantic in a kayak we were to say later). When we reached Phoenix, we registered at the Arizona Biltmore under the gold-leafed ceiling. Leonard's mouth hung open. "I feel I've died and gone to heaven," he said. We were inside one of Frank Lloyd Wright's great buildings—much like, we were told, his Imperial Hotel in Tokyo, long since demolished. The frontispiece of Eva Weber's *Art Deco in America* (1985) is a striking photo of an ornamental window wall in the Biltmore, designed by Wright in 1927. Its abstract pastel geometric design gleams against the dull pressed brick found throughout the resort complex.

For two months after our visit to the Arizona Biltmore, having met with Deco buffs all over the country and having been shown a staggering number of Deco architectural treasures—from great skyscrapers and ornate theatres to humble main streets—in a range of styles, we processed our slides of the trip, and eventually in 1981 we stood before three hundred Chicago designers in the beautiful Prairie Style lecture hall of the Architectural Foundation. It was a rapt audience, amazed at the extent and beauty of American Deco, aghast at the demolition of the New Yorker Hotel, delighted with the insights we furnished about our own District. We had them all the way—until we came to Frank Lloyd Wright and the Arizona Biltmore. What derision! What shock! Wright a Deco architect? Never! Only an ignorant sensation-monger would associate Chicago's Frank Lloyd Wright with the bizarre European style called Art Deco! Yet, were we so wrong in linking Wright to the Art Deco style? Time and further study may exonerate us, for, increasingly, Wright's work is shown in exhibits and illustrated in books as being integral to early Art Deco style.

The Skyscraper Style

When the members of the original group of architects arrived in Miami, and as they were developing the Miami Beach style that was to culminate in 1941, three Art Deco building types were proliferating across the country. One was the skyscraper. Second was the movie house seen everywhere, from the sophisticated Trans-Lux chain in the cities to the Fox and Paramount and other individually owned theatres that brought glamour to the smallest towns. The third, fast disappearing as parkways and through-ways predominated, was Deco roadside architecture, the subject of many books and exhibits in our Deco Revival era.

On our trip around the country, Leonard Horowitz and I, approaching cities situated off to the side of the parkways and bridges beyond the industrial murk of the outskirts, would see differentiated from the solid mass of tall buildings comprising the contemporary skyline one or more graceful spired or stepped-shape silhouettes. We would turn off the throughway and pierce the city aiming for that spire, secure in the assumption that it would be an important Art Deco building.

We had been tipped off about the Baton Rouge, Lousiana, state capitol by the architect son of Joseph Dreyfus, the original architect, then at work on the plans for the New Orleans World's Fair of 1984. We could see the capitol presiding over the city from far off. It was, of course, Huey Long's monumental achievement of 1934. We went to the observatory, twenty-six stories up, to look down on Long's grave in an orderly green park, and to discover the marvelous Deco grille on the elevator tower, a frieze with a lightning bolt and crescent moon, a design later adapted by Leonard for a District project. The lobby, with walls and floors of marble, features a gift from the French government to Louisiana, a Sèvres porcelain urn, like the huge urns that had surrounded the Sèvres Pavilion at the 1925 Paris exposition.

We saw other skyscrapers that took our breath away with their grandeur: the Bullock's-Wilshire department store in Los Angeles; the Chicago Board of Trade building with its black corbels and silver-relief sculptures, and where Ceres, the goddess of agriculture, a small sculptured figure on the tower, stands guard over La Salle Street.

Guided by members of Allied Arts of Seattle, who had already published their splendid booklet, *Art Deco Seattle*, we stood reverently in two other temples of commerce, the Exchange Building and the Seattle Tower—their entrance lobbies having dazzling gold Art Deco ornament set against dark

Steven Brooke's spectacular photograph of this Collins Avenue streetscape highlights the Art Deco resort beauty of three hotels all designed by L. Murray Dixon: left to right, the Senator (1939) at 1201 Collins, the Kent (1939) at 1131, and the Palmer House (1936) at 1119.

The Webster, a charming small hotel across the street from the Senator at 1220 Collins Avenue, was designed by Hohauser in 1936.

The Alamac at 1300 Collins Avenue, now completely remodeled by Mel Schlusser as a condominum with apartments, was designed by V. H. Nellenbogen in 1934. Sender, Tragash, Architects designed the exemplary remodeling.

46

This remarkable Hohauser building at 1450 Collins, when it was designed in 1939, was Hoffman's Cafeteria, then later became the Warsaw Ballroom. After many years of being closed, it reopened as Club Ovo in 1987, a synthesis of new architectural decor and Woody Vondracek's pastel treatment of the exterior with its "angel wing" curves sweeping from a central turret. Now repainted black and gold on the exterior, the disco has now become the China Club, with that chain's traditional blue, Sino-American decor.

polished stone—described as reminiscent of movie palaces of the twenties.

We were to see that other great Deco state capitol building, in North Dakota's Bismarck, created by the leading architects of the Midwest, Holabird and Root of Chicago. A stripped-style building, this, like the Board of Trade in Chicago, had immense rows of shining bronze chandeliers, shaped like sheaves of wheat, set against tall corridors of white marble.

In Minnesota's Twin Cities our guide was Charles Senseman, a prolific collector and designer, who had moved from Miami to Minneapolis in 1980. We toured a series of Deco towers there with memorable reliefs and sculptures, all connected with the city's skywalk. It was the skyscraper city hall in St. Paul, however, that was the most astounding. The lobby was dominated by an American Indian god of peace that was two stories high and slowly revolved. Carved in green onyx by Swedish sculptor Carl Milles, it was a gift of the Mexican government to the city.

Impressive skyscraper lobbies are to be found in many major cities. In 1983, having been invited to help inaugurate the recycling of the Union Depot in Tulsa, Oklahoma, as an office building and the preservation of this neo-Gothic landmark in the middle of downtown, I was shown a series of splendid thirties office buildings set among recent buildings, replete with gilded coffered ceilings and custom chandeliers and marble walls.

In Tulsa the skyscraper that most excited me, however, was a church, the Boston Avenue Methodist church designed by Bruce Goff, which, says David Gebhard in his preface to *Art Deco Tulsa*, "at dusk could be the embodiment of Hugh Ferris's skyscraper renderings." Its soaring 225-foot tower emerges from setbacks and other towers in a display of Mayan verticality. The chime loft, at the first setback of the tower, is sheathed in copper and ends in a steel-and-glass finial of four fins, designed, says Gebhard, to reflect light in dramatic patterns.

The New York skyscraper was the basic inspiration for late-thirties architecture in Miami Beach. In his book *The Skyscraper*, Paul Goldberger, architectural critic for *The New York Times*, wrote eloquently about the Chrysler building with its white brick tower trimmed in gray brick and with gargoyles resembling the 1929 Chrysler automobile hood ornaments, and the stainless steel arches culminating in a giant spire. "The Chrysler," says Goldberger, "goes beyond Art Deco to become a truly new kind of skyscraper. Its bizarre form seems a perfect encapsulation of the energy and flamboyance of Manhattan at the end of the 1920's."

It was this energy, this flamboyance, that Hohauser

and Dixon brought with them from New York. They were concerned with three- and four- and, at most, ten-story buildings, but New York's skyscrapers certainly influenced their approach.

Another great building for architects of the time was the Philadelphia Savings Fund Society building (PSFS), designed by George Howe and William Lescaze, completed in 1932. Considered by Goldberger to be a forerunner of the International Style, the building was considered powerfully modernistic. Many of the District's little buildings were to borrow from the PSFS: for example, the horizontal strip windows; and seen in microcosm in the small apartment buildings, windows abutting at the corners, which were cantilevered and shaded the floor below. Maxwell Levinson, George Howe's student, and editor of *Shelter* in the thirties, was to work with us by lecturing, editing Art Deco Society publications, and organizing the Philadelphia Art Deco Society.

It probably seems a wild idea to relate these small resort hotels of Miami Beach to the giant towers proliferating in the cities, but an important architectural motif contributes to the homogeneous character of the historic district: the attempt to simulate the skyward reaching, spired, towered effect of the great skyscrapers. Small hotels and the little apartment buildings on the back residential streets—Euclid, Jefferson, and Meridian—echo this theme over and over. There is usually the grand entrance, which is pulled together at the center of the building to carry the eye to the pylon or tower design at the top. The wings on either side are subdued, simply extending the horizontal line to offer a contrast to the elaborate center.

The ornamental devices that dramatize the entrance and towers draw on all the popular Deco themes. There are Mayan vegetative friezes and plaques, Moorish twisted columns, artful working of shadows with scalloped ledges to cast a curving line over the doors, and the use of the most advanced technological materials, such as glass block, Vitrolite, chrome, fluted pillars, and columns of raked concrete.

It was ornament of the types just described that reflected the skyscrapers, and it was combined with the modest use of keystone to simulate the marble in the great skyscraper lobbies, or with stucco to capture the smoothness of granite. The chrome, the ornamental shapes of the balustrades, the jewel-like sconces with their cut glass, the shining aluminum and chrome masts, and the neon were meant to capture the excitement of the new skyscrapers.

Also like the skyscrapers—self-promoting and

aggressive in the tight space of large cities—our buildings employ signage as decoration. Pylons, fins, and spires become advertising signboards. Stylish graphics in the terrazzo of porches and lobbies identify and promote the hotels. The use of lettering as an architectural element reflected the delight that the architects took in modern styles of display, a fine example being the name *Cavalier* applied to the facade of the hotel.

Corner buildings like Dixon's Senator, Tudor, and Tiffany on Collins, or the Abbey, Plymouth, and Adams on 21st Street, are particularly suggestive of the skyscraper style with their spires and perpendicular thrust, and the ribbon windows that wrap around the curving corners. "Short skyscrapers" or "skyscraperettes" they have been called.

Increasingly in our Deco Revival period, Art Deco architectural style is described as being "Mayan," yet before a book by Marjorie Ingle called *Mayan Revival Style, Art Deco Mayan Fantasy* was published in 1984, this was a term used only by scholars.

The Mayan style was widely used in the Deco years, particularly in New York's skyscrapers. Ely Jacques Kahn's design for the Two Park Avenue Building, or the twin towers of the Waldorf-Astoria hotel with Mayan revival-style ornamentation, "was a subtle sign of their pyramidal identity" says Ingle. Ancient stepped pyramids of the Maya and Aztec cultures in Mexico offered a vehicle for modern American architecture, and skyscrapers with setbacks and Mexican stepped pyramids became linked in people's minds.

Frank Lloyd Wright, Marion Griffin, and Francis Barry Byrne were among the distinguished architects who pursued the style in residences, stores, and theatres. They experimented with early forms of cast concrete and stark shapes, particularly in the Los Angeles area. Wright took the style to Tokyo in 1916 for his Imperial Hotel, and Griffin experimented with concrete block in the Precolumbian style in Australia. However, it was the Californian Robert P. Stacy-Judd who was the most ardent exponent of and is most credited with the Mayan revival. Stacy-Judd wore Mayan costumes and lectured and published widely on Mayan culture. He undertook two expeditions to Mexico, and his work appeared in architectural journals and the popular press. His most important structure was the Aztec Hotel built in 1925 in Monrovia, California, which at the time was described as "the first attempt ever made to modernize this pre-historic culture." Such was Stacy-Judd's influence that Mayan and Aztec homes, theatres, churches, and pyramidal skyscrapers flourished throughout the U.S.

The Influence of Hollywood Revisited

One of the important factors that fueled the Deco Revival was the enormous role of the movies as mirrors of period style and of the theatres that were the concomitants of film-industry development. A large show from the Smithsonian Institution in Washington, D.C., toured museums in 1986. It was called *Hollywood: Legend and Reality*. This show was developed from a series of studies, books, and memorabilia collections, and it drew on the new interest in old movies created by reruns on television as cable TV and VCRs proliferated. Included in the exhibition and accompanying the 256-page book was a variety of fascinating material. A model of a set design from *The Thief of Baghdad* (1924) focused attention on the Moorish fantasies from which Florida's astonishing Opa-Locka was derived. Busby Berkeley's *Gold Diggers of 1933* provided a neon violin from one of its lavish production numbers. Design sketches, costumes, props, and posters revivified the aesthetic and cultural impact of the film industry on our society. This influential exhibition opened at the Smithsonian Museum of American History in Washington, traveled to the Cooper-Hewitt Museum in New York City, came on to us in Miami at the Center for the Fine Arts, and then went to Cincinnati, Denver, and Los Angeles.

Herbert Scherer, a University of Minnesota art historian, and a frequent lecturer to the Art Deco Society, published an article called "Marquees on Main Street" in Mitchell Wolfson, Jr.'s scholarly quarterly, *Decorative and Propaganda Arts*, in which he reviewed the work of a regional architect, Jack Liebenberg, who can serve as an excellent example for what dozens of architects were doing simultaneously throughout the world. Liebenberg built and remodeled two hundred movie theatres in the upper Midwest. Scherer paints a vivid portrait of the midwestern downtown during the Depression: worn, drab, and dispirited. The "insertion" of the sleek, shining movie theatres became heartening symbols of the better times to come on those sad Main Streets. Liebenberg, a typical regional architect, was a Harvard graduate and winner of the Prix de Rome. He was like many unsung architects who quietly changed the face of the country, yet were not credited by their peers. A Minneapolis TV station—with Scherer—has produced a wonderful film on Liebenberg's theatres, so he finally has received well-deserved appreciation for his "little jewel boxes of modernism."

Through Scherer's article one soon realizes that the movie house became as important to the Deco

One of the District's supreme examples of the streamlined style is yet unrestored: the 1941 Haddon Hall, by L. Murray Dixon, set back from the street with a curving drive and statuary at 1500 Collins.

The St. Moritz, 1565 Collins, a landmark building set on a knoll, was last alive in 1984 when a summerfest conducted by MDPL thrilled patrons in its atmospheric dining room. Designed by Roy F. France in 1939, it is rumored to be a target by the same developers demolishing other hotels on that block.

The Berkeley Shore, 1610 Collins, by Albert Anis in 1940, is not protected by the city designation. It is, perhaps, the most fanciful building designed by Anis. Note the handsome floral plaques.

Burger King's Deco Revival branch on Lincoln Road at Collins has broken records in sales even though it has no parking lot or drive-through. It carries on the tradition of White Towers in a tropical way.

Here are the tall Delano and National hotels on Collins Avenue at 1685 and 1687, respectively. The National, topped by a domelike templetto now painted silver, was designed by Roy F. France in 1940. The Delano was built later in 1947 by Swartburg, and it is generally likened to a Buck Rogers space creation because of the fanciful wing projections on the tower. The Roosevelt family maintained a penthouse here for many years.

The Surfcomber, at 1717 Collins, was a 1948 latecomer by MacKay & Gibbs, but Leonard Horowitz's palette links its almost-fifties lines with an earlier, softer style.

style as the skyscraper, perhaps even more so because of its ubiquity. In 1981, on our tour around the country, Leonard Horowitz and I saw how a new interest was bringing the thirties theatres back to glowing life. In Spokane, Washington, where the city hall is a recycled Deco Montgomery Ward warehouse, the architects who had done the conversion were spearheading a drive to spruce up a wonderful Fox Theatre that is almost as elaborate as the Paramount in Oakland, California, which has become, like New York's Radio City Music Hall, a Deco shrine.

The work of Miami Beach's architectural team was not so much influenced by the Deco movie houses as it was part of the same thinking that produced them. In the Plymouth and the Abbey on 21st Street or Dixon's tower-dominated hotels on Collins, the motion-picture house aesthetic—the combination of streamlining, speed suggested by horizontality, and the self-advertising spire and signage—were part of the wave of popular commercial Deco.

Roadside America and Industrial Design

The great exhibition devoted to industrial design called "The Machine Age 1918-1941," which opened at The Brooklyn Museum in New York October 7, 1986, was to the end of the Deco Revival period what the landmark "World of Art Deco" exhibition held at The Minneapolis Institute of Arts in 1971 was to its beginning. It caused people to think anew about their environment—from the humblest household objects to the tallest skyscrapers. Richard Guy Wilson, a frequent lecturer in the District, and Dianne H. Pilgrim, a curator at The Brooklyn Museum, were the authors of the exhibition's important book and organizers of the exhibit.

John Russell, art critic for *The New York Times*, said:

> We see a great country coming to terms with technological advances that were to change life in its every least detail. But the show is also about faith and hope, at a moment in history that encourages neither of them, and about American readiness to get up and go, American stoicism and American sass...it is the revelation of a great and poignant moment in American affairs.

Wilson, including in the book photographs of our New Yorker and Century hotels, wrote: "a major factor is the emergence of the sleek, streamlined body, the machine in motion." Wilson traces the impetus for architectural streamlining to the early 1930s and Norman Bel Geddes, an industrial designer and architect, who combined aspects of International Style—strip windows, the color white, and pipe railings—with the rounded fins used for facades and canopies. Bel Geddes's residences impart an air of the nautical efficiency of a large liner with sheer hulls and a superstructure.

"Streamlining in American architecture was generally restrained, a curving wall or two, a little pipe-railing," says Wilson. But with Kem Weber, an industrial designer in southern California, streamlining became more aggressive. Its zenith was reached, perhaps, in Robert Derrah's 1937 Coca-Cola bottling plant in Los Angeles, which replicated a huge landlocked ship with a bridge, portholes, bulkhead doors, ships' ladders, and large ventilators. The cleanliness implied by the nautical style was an early attempt to clean up Coke's image, for it was frequently attacked as being impure and unhealthy.

In 1985, Chesler H. Liebes published *Main Street to Miracle Mile: American Roadside Architecture*, a book that reflected the popular enthusiasm for diners, pop-culture restaurants with signs and buildings shaped like beagles, ducks, or milk bottles, and even Art Deco gas stations. The automobile and the hunger for movement had fast developed wayside commerce.

Liebes's view is that Art Deco was a twenties style used for architectural detailing on a host of downtown buildings, but it was Streamlined Moderne, in contrast to Art Deco, which appealed to the designers of roadside architecture in the thirties. "The buildings for the roadside were designed with rounded corners and detailed with lines of flow suggesting motion. Modern materials enhanced the effect. Structural glass and porcelain, and stainless enameled metal panels made walls smooth and gleaming; stainless steel provided futuristic accents, and glass blocks were built into glowing, translucent yet structural windows."

Industrial designers like Raymond Loewy, Gordon Lippincott, Donald Deskey, and Walter Dorwin Teague were among the first wave of industrial designers to develop prototypes for mass-produced gas stations and restaurant chains, thereby putting their modern imprint on the American landscape.

The realization that such industrial commercial designs belonged in the realm of art history and serious study was most welcome to preservationists in Miami. It was a major tool for persuading the public that our modest pop-culture little hotels were an aspect of the aesthetic achievement of machine-age America. It was now much more possible for design critics to elaborate on the "beauty" of the District.

My own experience from the fifties to the early

seventies as a market researcher for the great designers, Loewy, Deskey, Lippincott, and their clients, the giant corporations, had made me aware of the design process. I had watched how gas stations, cars, restaurants, and trademarks were transformed to respond to sociological and cultural changes, always keeping those almost subliminal familiar features that were special and memorable. I had seen the production line in the large offices of the design firms operated as designs moved from one designer's carrel to another, slowly, almost impersonally, changing to conform to the perceived needs made clear by predesign research.

Industrial designers still produce prototypes for gas stations. But reawakened sensibilities sometimes request chains to retain the Deco style. In Coral Gables in 1982, a struggle was waged to convince Gulf to keep its gas station designed by Russell Pancoast in the thirties. It has columns that look machine turned, from which at the top cloud formations sweep across the station bay. These Deco themes are set off by barrel-tiled roofs, a transitional design that marked Pancoast's district hotels like the Peter Miller. A spirited campaign convinced the company's district sales manager that sometimes local identity and preferences are more valuable than corporate identity.

The same new regard now being lavished on the fast-food chains of the thirties has been directed to another roadside phenomenon, the diner. Author and Superrealist painter, John Baeder, a supporter of the District from the beginning, is prominently connected with the special interest in diners as a significant aspect of Americana, and he has even designed a line of tableware inspired by them.

The architecture of our Art Deco District might then be said to have its real roots in the "low" style of mass marketing of the thirties. The pylons with signage, the self-advertising fantasy, the sweeping overhangs, and dramatic parapets all share a common vocabulary with roadside architecture of the machine age. To fault the District architecture for its lack of "high" Deco sculpture, grandiose scale, and rich marble, silver, and gold is seriously to miss the point. The true significance of our buildings is not their materials or ornaments but the way that they capture so strikingly the dynamic, Modernist spirit of the machine age.

Case Histories—A Balance Sheet

What follows is a review of some of the successes of the District: the revitalized streets and buildings. It also discusses the contradictory trends: the erosion of historic detail versus the gaining of new markets (e.g., the thousands of young people who come to the District for dancing and entertainment); the opportunity to exist proudly as a living textbook of thirties domestic architecture versus the need for investors to find a profit on the bottom line. Here it can be learned how our decade of struggle was to enhance the District—as we were the true guardians of its treasures—and how we sometimes lost the struggle.

The Main Post Office and Murals

The Main Post Office on Washington Avenue and 12th Street came to public attention before the Deco District was declared. It appeared in Martin Grieff's book *Depression Modern* (1975). Its circular form, elegant rotunda tower, use of keystone steps and door framing, all placed it clearly in the new idiom. Yet we found it in decrepit condition in 1977. A fortunate series of incidents: an ASID conference in Washington, D.C.; a group of designers from MDPL; the presence of my younger son, John, in Washington that summer with a coterie of young friends; and a wonderful party at the new home of preservation, the glorious U.S. Pension Building, about to be restored by our friend Chris Delaporte, new head of the preservation movement, brought us together. The secretary of GSA (General Services Administration), the government's maintenance bureau for its buildings, spoke to the designers' party. "If you have any buildings at home that you think should be saved, tell us. We want to save our heritage," he said. All of us clustered around a stranger from GSA, a charming young architect, and told him about our Depression Moderne Washington Avenue post office. He had read of Miami Beach Deco in *Preservation News*.

When I returned to Miami a week later, there was a message for me: "Call the post office!" A team of government architects had been there and were ready to go ahead.

Thus began the first restoration project in the District, a 1937 example of the "stripped" classical style used throughout the nation for schools, city halls, and a variety of public buildings, where labor was supplied by government programs. The post office appointed a local architect for the restoration and asked him to work with a committee from MDPL. Our best design members served on it. Great care was taken to design a new ramp for wheelchairs, and new balustrades that would enhance and yet conform to the design. The correct chemicals were discussed for cleaning the keystone and the brass lockboxes so that they would not be discolored or scratched. Plant materials were discussed with our

Looking south on Collins, here is an impressive lineup of hotels. The Richmond, South Seas, Marseilles, Del Caribe, Ritz Plaza, Surfcomber, and Delano.

The Shelborne, 1801 Collins, was designed by Igor B. Polevitsky in 1954. The fourteen-story building, with its ribbon windows and impressive verticals, is considered a forerunner of the International Style. A full-scale hotel and residence, it has been kept in continuous operation. The signage is particularly handsome.

The South Seas, 1751 Collins, by L. Murray Dixon, 1941.

Hotel del Caribe, 1725 Collins, another postwar hotel by MacKay & Gibbs, 1948.

The Raleigh, 1777 Collins, with ribbon windows in its broad rounded corner is a Dixon masterpiece that opened in 1940. The fantasy bathhouse and the R monogram on the square tower help project a feeling of modernism.

The Greystone, 1926 Collins, by Henry Hohauser in 1939, was considered the apotheosis of District design, until an ill-designed store facade was placed in the corner of the first floor. The flagpoles and decorative discs and center pylon for signage all still evoke the fantasy of seaside architecture.

WASHINGTON
AVENUE

One of the earliest resort hotels, the George Washington stands unrestored at the entry to the architectural District, at 534 Washington Avenue. Striped awnings for the arched windows like those at Espanola Way are long gone but the fancy finals remain. How exciting it will be to bring back the early Beach days with this building designed by William P. Brown in 1924!

The City and County Revitalization Plan for Washington Avenue, which was designed by the firm of Venturi, Rauch & Scott-Brown, was the subject of a cover story in the December 1982 issue of *Progressive Architecture*. The article was illustrated with this photograph of Friedman's Bakery at 685 Washington Avenue and with the one used as the frontispiece for this book on page 2. *Life* and *Avenue* magazines used Friedman's as a centerpiece in pioneering fashion articles with the District in the background. Friedman's Bakery has now become Watergun, repainted in black and gold, where antique clothing is sold.

Your Everything Store at 659 Washington Avenue. A detail photograph of the store's handsome wall is illustrated on page 10.

The Famous, a noted Jewish restaurant on Washington Avenue, was gutted to create the District's most popular restaurant, The Strand, with architecture by Yosse Friedman.

The Blackstone, at 800 Washington Avenue, represents the most striking victory for a long struggle to provide improved housing for the elderly. D. Kingstone Hall's fourteen-story Mediterranean structure of 1929, remodeled in 1934 with V. H. Nellenbogen as architect, now holds 131 apartments. E. Santos, AIA, of Chisholm, Santos & Ramundez, recovered delightful courtyards, a clay-tile sweeping staircase, and retained the rough-textured stucco interior walls. The developers, Related Housing, reopened the resort hotel to meaningful new grandeur in 1988.

The Taft and Kenmore, at 1044 and 1050 Washington Avenue, respectively, blend together because the same owner used Leonard Horowitz's colors in one of the earliest remodeling efforts. Both were built in 1936; the Taft designed by Henry Hohauser, and the Kenmore, by Anton Skislewicz. The Kenmore's neon-lighted staircase with sensuous railings has been a strong draw for the press.

landscape architects. A tile maker worked for a year to produce the blue barrel tile for the roof, and the exact color was a subject of agonizing decision.

Later, I was to stand in the long line that always forms at this post office, thinking of the unsung heroes who had made the new air-conditioning possible. Old rotten wood and walls had been stripped out and the blessed air-conditioning was considered essential to proper maintenance. I enjoyed also running my hands over the marble Directoire-Deco stamp tables with their decorations of Roman fasces, marveling that these had been saved. I was to learn at Micky Wolfson's Italian exhibit at his new Museum of Decorative and Propaganda Arts that the fasces, a popular Fascist symbol throughout Italy, had been a Deco motif from the beginning.

Today MDPL tours always go into the post office to see the Charles Hardin mural in the rotunda. Typically this WPA narrative-realist work has scenes of Indians and cavalry. Unfortunately, the post office made the mistake of not allotting proper maintenance funds for the fountains—the large one in the rotunda and the charming dolphin fountain were never turned on. Nevertheless, this restoration was a huge step forward not only for Miami Beach but also for the nation. Our Washington Avenue post office, a $400,000 restoration, was said to be the first instance of a Deco post office and its mural having been saved.

Murals and the District

The surviving muralists, now in their late seventies, who came to Miami from New York in the thirties recall the exciting world of ideas and fun that marked the District, much like today's gatherings where young artists and designers are at all the parties and openings here. Earl LaPan and Paul Silverthorne tell how they worked in the trolley-car barns at the foot of the island and on location by day, and gambled and danced in the new nightclubs around John Collins Park (where the Bass Museum and library are) by night.

At the Colony Hotel one sees the influence of the work of Mexico's Diego Rivera in a mural above a fireplace surrounded by shiny green Vitrolite. Peeling back layers of paint at the Cardozo Hotel, we uncovered large abstract shapes that stretched across the ceiling. At the Royal Palm Hotel great Deco flowers were discovered under wallpaper in the lobby. Still found in hotels like the Victor are a mural by LaPan, and his other flamingo mural is at the Hotel Flamingo. At first it had been common to dismiss his work as fuddy-duddy naturalism, but a closer

examination revealed LaPan's Impressionism: the soft pastels had the strength and painterliness of both the New York School, where he had been an apprentice to George Luks, and revealed his openness to the colors and techniques of the French. There were some three hundred murals painted by LaPan in Miami.

Meanwhile, the Deco Revival generation is once more filling the lobbies with mural art, ranging from the slapdash "Memphis" style in the Tropics Café at the Edison, to the careful and very-thirties scenes of resort life in the dining room of the Astor by Joyce Murray, which were commissioned by Leonard Horowitz in 1980. The Cuban painter, Raida, spent a year on the formal group mural in the lobby of the Breakwater, which features a large group of politicians and preservationists turning away a wrecking ball hovering over Ocean Drive, and lead by Gerry Sanchez, who commissioned the painting.

The Spanish Village and the Mediterranean Style

It seemed an overnight happening in 1986 when the Spanish Village of the seventies on Espanola Way emerged from decades of seediness as a neat, unified, striking, and very 1980s restoration. Between Washington and Euclid on 15th Place there are salmon-colored buildings with green-and-white striped awnings on one side, and with red-and-white on the other. Tantalizing entrances flanked by twisted columns and classical pediments, and views of garden courtyards seen from the narrow street, are a living tribute to the twenties village created by B.T. Roney, whose large Breakers-like resort, the Roney, was up at 24th Street.

Gerry Sanchez's Polonia Restoration company, the same group that had brought back the Edison Hotel, a classic in a similar genre, did the restoration. The design by young Randall Sender, AIA, and his associates leaned heavily on the original architects, Robert Taylor and L. Murray Dixon. The idea in 1926 was to create "an artists' colony where artists and lovers of the artistic might congregate amid congenial surroundings," the kind of place then lacking on the Beach, a place like Greenwich Village or the Latin Quarter in Paris, both in their heyday in the twenties.

Roney's grand hotel was the essence of a Mediterranean luxury resort, with canopied cabanas along a boardwalk. But he wanted "a miniature Spanish village for fiesta and song, mantillas and lace." The Spanish architecture employed was liberally laced with an eclectic mix of revival styles—Spanish, Moroccan, Italian, and French, as well as Art Deco.

Boutiques lined the street, selling antique jewelry, rare books, fine clothes, and furniture.

Obviously, Roney was motivated by Addison Mizener's Palm Beach fantasies. "Mizener," said Tom Austin in 1986, writing for the *Miami Review* at the time of the AIA Fantasy Design Conference in Miami, "was South Florida's fantasy architect. He had an idea that Spanish architecture, a style he had always favored, would ennoble the subtropical landscape of Palm Beach, and give it the civilizing aura of timelessness it needed."

Mizener's friend Paris Singer, heir to the sewing machine fortune, wanted to afford his guests some place to go in the evening so he concocted Worth Avenue with its narrow "vias modeled after old Spanish Villages."

The Miami Beach Spanish Village was built in 1922; Palm Beach's Worth Avenue in 1924. Austin repeats the often-told story of how Mizener fanatically made his buildings look old on the day they were finished:

> The doors of his mansions would be flayed with chains until they looked battered. Mizener would apply baking soda to poured concrete, pitting the surface, creating the weathered appearance of old stone. Walls were sprayed with condensed milk and then rubbed down with steel wool until their glossiness faded. He used pecky cypress, a wood that ages instantly for his ceilings. Woodite could be carved up and made to resemble antique moulding. Iron work was dipped in acid baths to give the impression of decay. If a mason's efforts were too polished he would simply hack off the edges with a hatchet. It was all a way of making the ready-made appear ancient, creating buildings that appeared to have been "in the family" for generations.

Randy Sender, not having the original blueprints, which were destroyed in a fire at the Miami Beach Building Department before Beach history became important, worked from the original photographs, which showed the rough stucco. "It looked ancient like Mizener," he said. It is, of course, more than probable that Mizener was enchanted by Roney's Spanish Village, two hours down the coast, already established as a playground for wealthy vacationers. Anyhow, antiquing new buildings was in the air. Bernhardt Mueller was doing it at another fantasy world for the elite: Opa-Locka, the Moorish Arabian Nights village being developed by Glenn Curtiss not far from Miami Beach. There the walls of the city hall were carefully distempered with patches of stucco artfully showing the lath beneath.

If Espanola Way was actually the inspiration for Mizener's dramatic eclectic style and Worth Avenue's flower and fountain-filled little courts, it is hardly as famous. The difference is that Palm Beach continued to value its fantasy, whereas Miami Beach with its eye to immediate profits moved northward to sanction the concrete canyon, abandoning Espanola Way to derelicts and drugs.

In 1977, when still living on Key Biscayne, I brought Linda Polansky, an aggressive twenty-three-year-old realtor, to Miami Beach. By 1978, she had collected enough backing to buy the Clay Hotel, the major building on the block. Repeatedly fighting off city-code officials, she struggled to revitalize Espanola Way and hit on the idea of inaugurating a youth hostel. Today, the Clay Hotel is a major stop for international young hikers and cyclists, and their presence in the red-tiled lobby and coffee shop is one of the most charming aspects of the new District.

The designation for Espanola Way makes special mention of the mix of architectural styles. Among Hohauser's streamlined modern buildings are 144 and 1450 Collins and 724 and 1735 Espanola Way. Roy France's 1440 Euclid and Carlos Schoepple's 446 Espanola are also Deco buildings. Robert Taylor abandoned his own version of a Spanish village to design 1440 Pennsylvania Avenue as the lastest word in architecture for his own residence and studio. Espanola Way, then, may be considered a prototype of the transition from the Mediterranean style to Deco.

Moresque and Mediterranean Revival

It has been something of an embarrassment to promoters of the Art Deco District that more than one third of it is composed of buildings that have their roots in an earlier time and place. They are usually described as being Mediterranean. What has not been clearly understood is that Spanish Colonial, Mediterranean, and even Pueblo (seen in small homes in the District around Flamingo Park) were all stylistic variations of early twentieth-century fantasy.

On the Beach there were faithful attempts to re-create the Italian style—most notable was the Amsterdam Palace, Henry LaPointe's reproduction of Christopher Columbus's home. But also on the residential streets little apartment buildings had Moroccan twisted columns, or as is the case with Hohauser's 1939 Park Vendome, Tuscan loggias with tiled fountains and recessed niches and grillwork.

The Riviera background of the Deco style, seen in the orange-red tiled roofs that hung over blue seas in canvases by Raoul Dufy, or in the brilliantly patterned interiors of Henri Matisse's Nice paintings of the twenties and thirties—these are the sources that filled

The Main Post Office, 1300 Washington Avenue, was illustrated in Martin Grief's book *Depression Modern* (1975). It was designed in the Deco Federal style by Howard L. Cheney in 1939. The wall mural by Charles Hardman and the ceiling design are in the rotunda.

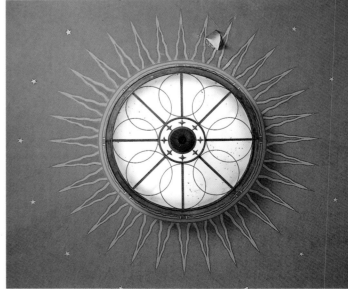

The Davis, 1020 Washington. Henry Hohauser dramatized the little hotel with a shiplike prow of glass block in 1941. The lobby has fine corbels and railings designed by the architect.

At 1001 Washington Avenue, the great Moorish-style Washington Storage Company with its Spanish Renaissance relief facade is a landmark at the Beach which was designed by Robertson and Patterson in 1927. In the thirties it was used to store furnishings that were used only during the two months of the season. The building is now being put to an exciting use by Mitchell Wolfson, Beach native, and his Wolfson Foundation, for it will house a collection of early twentieth-century art objects, paintings, and books, all available for use by students. The building is being modernized with dehumidification and security systems, and a clubhouse will be developed on the roof. The Matthews family, who owned the storage company from the beginning, is still involved and a source of pioneer stories. William Kearn, ASID, is the interior designer for the recycling.

Owned by the Brandt family, Club 1235 at 1235 Washington, brings back some of the craftsmanship and glamour of the original French Casino designed by Thomas Lamb in 1936. The drama of the original is captured by Steven Brooke's exciting photographs of the lobby, with the original chandelier, staircase, and striking balcony design. Club names and ownership change, but the basic beauty remains.

Old City Hall is another early public building at 1130 Washington Avenue. Designed by Deco architect Martin Luther Hampton in 1927, it was considered a nine-story testimonial to a glowing future for the Beach after the great hurricane of 1926. Neoclassical Corinthian columns, urn finials, and barrel-tile roofing give it grandeur. Lovingly articulated by Stuart Grant and Randall Sender, AIA, then starting their careers as preservation architects, it was completed in 1987 along with the all-new, post-modern police station, its neighbor behind it, where Hohauser's beautiful Neron Hotel and a block of apartments were destroyed.

The 30's Promenade, 1201 Washington, a mini-mall conversion from a former Kress building, was developed in 1983, and it is now the headquarters for the Miami Design Preservation League's Welcome Center. Ron Molko's restoration of the keystone facade was the first major rehabilitation of important building materials, and the building's new use was seen as the beginning of a Washington Avenue renaissance. The block-long building, with its striking curving corner, originally had a central tower with a fountain motif over a marquee to the French Casino that was not replaced when it toppled in 1984.

The Cameo Theatre, at 1445 Washington and facing Espanola Way, was designed in 1938 by Robert Collins. It is noted for the carved keystone with its flourish of palm fronds framing a cameo portrait. The facade is a lively example of the eclecticism of Deco style, combining ornamental carvings with the spare modernism of the fluted columns and glass block. This is one of three remaining movie houses in the District where films may still be seen.

the architects' minds at the same time as Streamlined Moderne. Mediterranean styles on the Beach owe a great deal to the first builders and architects for Coral Gables, particularly Kiehnel and Elliott, the same firm that later designed the striking Art Deco Carlyle Hotel.

At the same time, throughout Greater Miami other fantasy buildings were going up. At Opa-Locka and Hialeah the inventor/aviator millionaire Glenn Curtiss was planning whole developments. The style for Hialeah was Pueblo, inspired by his visits to the Southwest. There were thick walls of cement block covered with hand-applied molded stucco. Curtiss next turned to Opa-Locka, where he constructed an airport for his friends—stunt flyers and other inventors—to enjoy. Indeed, it was from there that Amelia Earhart began her famous last journey, during which she disappeared. Opa-Locka was the place into which Curtiss was to pour all his ingenuity and financial resources before the devastating hurricane of 1926 and the end of the land boom, the Depression, and finally his own death in 1932. But through the early years, his fantasies along with those of his New York architect, Bernhard Mueller, developed into a gleaming white, Moresque, Arabian Nights village. Curtiss staged a publicity stunt to bring his Arabian vision to public attention. When the first train, loaded with dignitaries, arrived at the domed and minaretted railroad station, Curtiss and his friends were there to meet them, dressed in Arabian clothes and mounted on horses. From that colorful ceremony has developed today's Arabian Nights Festival complete with camels, elephants, and a parade of marching bands.

Today, Opa-Locka's city hall has been restored, all five domes having been reconstructed. The hotel is being recycled and restored, even though its roof was completely gone. The reconstruction architects were Les Beilinson, AIA, responsible for so many District restorations and a member of the Miami Beach Historic Preservation Board, and Thorn Grafton, AIA, grandson of Russell Pancoast and codesigner with Bernard Zyscovitch of the 21st Street Community Center in the Art Deco District.

At the successful Arabian Nights Festival in 1986, a show featured Moresque fashions by Humps of Bal Harbor, a boutique now taken over by Laise Adzer of Morocco. Against the turrets and domes of Glenn Curtiss's city hall these styles took on new meaning. Later on, a charity "Arabian Night" costume party celebrating Paul Poiret, the famous French couturier of the early twentieth century, was held at the District nightclub called Ovo (now the China Club) to raise funds for rebuilding Opa-Locka.

The Art Deco Hotels

Called the Art Deco Hotels, there was, beginning with the Cardozo in 1979, a group of seven hotels (the Victor, the Leslie, the Ocean View Apartments, the Carlyle, the Senator, and the Cavalier) that became the prime nucleus of the first wave of development in the Art Deco district.

The first Art Deco Weekend in October 1978 took place in the Cardozo, which was in my opinion the jewel of Ocean Drive. Run as a hotel for retirees, it was in sad shape, but even in 1978 I thought, "What will we do if we lose the Cardozo?" It was the sturdy lavender keystone pillars and the sweep of the overhanging curving porch roof that aroused my love for this building. I was later entranced by the front and rear sections of the building, and the staircase was like an Archipenko construction! Then there were the glass blocks, the handsome bosses, and the lobby with a succession of riches such as the bronze elevator door with a relief of tropic birds and the telephone booth with a circular window. Presided over by Earl LaPan's stern portrait of Supreme Court Justice Benjamin Cardozo, Jewish justice in the Roosevelt court, the Cardozo Hotel became the heart of our Art Deco activity. The Cardozo had been designed by Hohauser, and I came to fear it would be lost, because for a long while it seemed as if it were only Hohauser buildings that got torn down. We had lost Hohauser's round bar, the El Chico; there was talk at this time of losing the New Yorker; and we were to lose the Neron although I didn't know that yet—all works of this fine architect, the one probably closest in spirit to the Post-Modernists, who forty years later were to use Le Corbusier-like motifs: the oculus windows (we called them "portholes"), the round shining bosses, the pipestem railings, but most particularly the flowing curves of buildings designed like great boats on land: Nautical Moderne we were to call the style—sculptural, curvaceous, streamlined.

My son Andrew purchased the Cardozo in 1979 in the months preceding its nomination to the National Register of Historic Places, and he sought for limited partners to become investors in the first Art Deco hotel to be restored and run as a transient hotel on Miami Beach. The project was officially backed by the Miami Design Preservation League. After three years of promise and conjecture, our group, until then viewed as impractical idealists, had a very real and very practical cause celèbre. Hardly ever has one small hotel—it had seventy rooms—attracted so much media attention and discussion.

A large group of us traveled to Washington to

secure grants and loans promised by government planners when we were attempting to generate support for the nomination to the Register. The secretary of Housing and Urban Development (HUD), the Chief of the National Register, and young Deco buffs from all over Washington crowded hearing rooms and gasped with delight at our slides of dazzling white Moderne buildings photographed against the clear blue skies of tropical Miami. It was to take two years to consummate a loan agreement for restoration through the Economic Development Authority (EDA), and when it came the offer was not accepted by the local banks, who decided that nothing profitable would ever happen in that deteriorated neighborhood.

There was an aura about all that happened at the Cardozo, which soon was illustrated in magazines throughout the country, because so many people cared, and the idea had so much novelty. Beautiful things happened: Sunday-afternoon chamber music, with the sun-filled ocean and the boats getting dim beyond the big plate-glass windows; late-night impromptu performances when the professional group at the Fontainebleau's Art Deco La Ronde room came to clown around for their friends; weekends when restauranteur David Harrison would sit at his favorite table in the curve of the porch chatting with endless numbers of friends across the keystone balustrade; sunny mornings when the tablecloths were spread for breakfast, and writers John Rothchild and Jock McClintock would read their papers and talk, guilty about not being in their offices.

There were endless discussions about how to decorate. Should the halls be scraped to their Dade County pine base and then have Aubusson strip carpeting put down? Should bedspreads be chenile, as in thirties seashore hotels, or made from patterned chintz in a formal Deco pattern? Would it be possible in those early days of neon revival to commission an indoor piece for the hotel bar? Would it be possible to entice the noted wax-relief artist who visited the Cardozo to make an impression of the elevator door and then use this for a fabric design?

At its peak the Cardozo had regular combos playing on the porch and indoors; the little café spilled over into the lobby because tables were in such demand; the dull brown of the walls, when the hotel was acquired, were scraped to discover the right soft pink from the past; and a dessert counter reminiscent of Rumpelmayer's in Paris in the thirties was installed. Photographs of the *Bremen* and the *Normandie* were consulted to determine the best design for the glass vitrine that housed displays by Frances Carey, our local authority on thirties antiques.

The Carlyle Restored

Actually, the Cardozo had declined somewhat when the Carlyle reopened across the street. The Art Deco partners had renovated this one in the way they wanted to handle all six of their hotels on Ocean Drive. The world's largest hotel renovator, a Chicago firm, was hired and in three months on Art Deco Weekend in 1983, as scheduled, it was possible to throw a huge party at the restored hotel as the formal start to the weekend. All the rooms had been gutted; the furniture was new; the walls were smooth and the color fresh. Visitors were enticed to go to the windows and look at the ocean, which seemed so close, or to enjoy the view of the Cardozo across the street.

Once the Carlyle was open again it was always crowded. The regulars gathered at the bar each night. Young couples from Kendall, and older residents of Miami Beach mansions entertaining out-of-town guests with a tour of the District, felt somehow virtuous going to the Carlyle. They were striking a blow for Art Deco.

In the lobby Margaret Doyle had installed long full-length green curtains to match the black and green bar, which had been the hotel's reception desk. There was constant discussion of the green: it was a poor color for a bar, it would cast a green shadow on faces, the draperies were not a Deco color. This all stopped the day Michael Graves, the noted Post-Modern architect, attended a book and author luncheon at the Carlyle and pronounced them charming.

The Victor for Entertainment

The Victor was different. An eight-story highrise, it offered a glamorous view and it became the entertainment hotel.

After its thirty-two chandeliers and sconces had been cleaned by Ziggurat, a company formed by MDPL members to restore Art Deco antiques; after the LaPan mural had been cleaned; and after the terrazzo long hidden by carpeting had been exposed and shined, the hotel began to use its ship's salon-shaped dining room for dances and shows. It was the scene of Comedy Woom performances, repertory theatre, parties for all the permanent guests of the hotel chain on holidays, and for meetings and lectures. Moon Over Miami dances took place there, and the University of Miami School of Architecture held an architectural costume party on Halloween.

ESPANOLA WAY

Steven Brooke's view of the rich detailing that makes Espanola Way a delight. Sculptured casts, arches with elaborate capitals, grillwork, striped awnings, and elegant paintwork were all designed by Robert Taylor in 1925 and restored by Polonia with design by Sender, Tragash & Alvarino in 1986.

PENNSYLVANIA AVENUE

1045 Pennsylvania Avenue, the first restoration of a Moresque facade, restored by the owners in 1981, is Henry J. Maloney's 1929 apartment building. Pastel colors brought out the pineapple finials, Corinthian capitals, and the Baroque curves of the parapet.

Another of Henry Hohauser's splendid buildings is 1211 Pennsylvania designed in 1939. It is a residence that was much abused and that is now being beautifully restored throughout. The towering palms framing the entrance interestingly mirror the slender supports for the balconies. From 1978 to 1985 District history was written here, for the author's home was here.

The Ed Lee Apartments on Pennsylvania Avenue by Henry Hohauser, built in 1936, blossom under new paint, with a series of curving ledges articulated in the reds and greens of Midwest Deco. An otherwise plain building has been made handsome with stripes emphasizing the balcony and entrance and a sensitive handling of the floral plaque above the door canopy.

Naturally, the students dressed to represent the Cardozo and the Tides, and there was the inevitable reproduction of the famous Beaux Arts party in New York in the twenties when the great architects wore their buildings. Also, during the hotel's five-year existence, from its purchase in 1979 to the sale of all seven hotels in 1984, the hotels' and District's activities were indivisible. The League's offices and store were located in the Art Deco Hotels properties; poolside parties were held at the Senator.

Meanwhile, the founding firm, called the Art Deco Hotels, whichfinally had one hundred limited partners, many of them preservationists, became increasingly troubled financially. Large debts had accumulated to lawyers, tax accountants, and for national advertising. The purchaser in 1984 was the Cavanaugh Company, which had a background in Florida land sales. Cavanaugh intended to operate the hotels as Art Deco gems, they told the press. They were going to spend 6 million dollars for restoration. This figure became 16 million, then 32 million. "They are long on promises, short on performance," commented the *Herald*. All the hotels were closed over a period of time, beginning in 1984 with the Cardozo and the Victor.

It took two years to reopen the Carlyle. The Victor, which is intended to be the big hotel on the block, with large dining rooms, stores, and maintenance facilities, is still boarded up—its streamlined lighting fixtures gone, the LaPan mural closed from sight.

In 1983, when the great environmental artist Christo created his startling "Surrounded Islands," the extraordinary pink oasis on Biscayne Bay, his headquarters was located in the Art Deco hotels on Ocean Drive. The Drive bustled with his assistants who came from around the world to help with the project. Impromptu parties took place in the Carlyle Grill. Museum directors from Oslo and Amsterdam table-hopped to greet gallery owners and critics from New York and Paris. A planeload of Japanese photographers flew in to join the tremendous press corps.

The long inaction around the closed Cardozo and Victor, and the new wave of developers below the original restored hotels south of the Victor—e.g., the Clevelander; Sanchez's Edison, Breakwater, and Waldorf Towers; the group of hotels operating as "The Adrian"; and the hotels owned by Tony Goldman with the Park Central as his flagship—have shifted the crowd scenes southward, including Art Deco Weekend, which keeps moving down Ocean Drive.

During the papal visit in September 1987 developer Gerry Sanchez invited some one thousand mostly Hispanic friends to meet visiting bishops. The flower-filled gazebo and pool of the Edison was the setting seen on all TV networks. A full moon, neon, and washes of light on the restored hotels contributed to a romantically festive scene, only somewhat familiar as the setting for countless episodes of "Miami Vice" as it was not dressed in the familiar Art Deco pinks and greens of the first years of the TV series.

Prize fights, concerts, and fireworks have all been held on the beach in front of the hotels, and the City has responded with a public-works program of widening all of Ocean Drive, creating a promenade. The consequence of this focus on mass events has been to make the Art Deco District a huge learning experience. Hundreds of thousands of people have looked upward, noting the curious "eyebrows" and "portholes" of the thirties buildings, getting a vivid sense of this other era.

Lincoln Road—Closer to the Preservation Dream

Friday night on Lincoln Road. The Sterling Building glows, its glass blocks illuminated with soft blue light, the cove above the new canopy casting light upward to show the undulating curves. A rose light shines from the second-floor windows of the Foundlings, a woman's club that is part of the million-dollar renovation provided by the Mitchell Wolfson, Jr., Foundation. Through the arcade a giant soft-green ceramic urn is reflected in the polished green and soft-pink terrazzo. The open shops, SoBeit and Sterling Signatures, galleries of furniture and decorative arts, sparkle and entice. Tables are set on the sidewalk mall in front of the lively restaurant Wet Paint and when there is a performance of the Miami City Ballet, the boys and girls of the dance corps relax gracefully at a table inside. Most of the galleries are open, and inside there are knots of people discussing the new works on display. Strollers on the mall stop to greet friends with mutual congratulations: "Did you ever think this would happen?" A big band plays in the shadow of the Arts Center.

Since the seventies, when the local branch of New York's fashionable Saks Fifth Avenue closed its doors, Lincoln Road has been the despair of the Lincoln Road Merchants Association and the city planners. Once known as "The Fifth Avenue of the South," Lincoln Road was a high-fashion center. When I came from New York to visit during the war, I could still return, on a train crowded with soldiers, wearing a pastel cotton-jersey print dress and a pink-feather cloche, the latest styles from smart shops on Lincoln Road. At its height during the thirties, Edith

1540 Pennsylvania, the Delano, has been a favorite from the onset of the Deco Revival movement. Its classic central massing enlivened by the ziggurated lighting sconces, reflecting in miniature Deco skyscrapers, also has a bold terrazzo pattern extending to the street. It is a pink and gray Deco delight designed by Robert Swartburg in 1947.

EUCLID AVENUE

This very Moderne building at 748 Euclid Avenue was designed by Gene Bayliss in 1939. It is also called the Minden Apartments.

The Rosebloom at 820 Euclid, designed by Roy F. France in 1939, is noted for the imposing entrance arch leading to the court. Notice the vertical striping of the facade and the stepped parapet.

The Denis at 841 Euclid was the first small building in the residential sector to be rehabilitated. The fluting in the parapet and in the columns framing the entrance give it a classic appearance. The Denis was designed by Arnold Southwell in 1938.

The Enjoie at 928 Euclid Avenue is a joyful confection of crisp white enlivened with Deco yellow, coral, and lavender. Designed by Albert Anis in 1935, it has six units designed by Henry J. Maloney that were added in 1936.

1110 Euclid, the Siesta. The white banding at the top emphasizes handsomely the turreted silhouette of this building. Designed by Edward A. Nolan in 1936.

1350 Euclid—the Claire Apartments—is a classic streamlined two-story building made taller by a high curving parapet designed by Henry Hohauser in 1938.

1600 Euclid. The Evelyn. Here is a detail of a Mayan-style relief, probably sculpted *in situ* against a fluted background over the doorway.

MERIDIAN AVENUE

One of the older Mediterranean-style buildings, the Palm Gardens at 760 Meridian Avenue, created by H. H. Mundy in 1923, has been the subject of an intensive and striking restoration. Its Italianate window frames, arches, and quoins like twisted rope stand out in white against the soft pink ground.

The Parkway, at 736 13th Street with sides along Meridian Avenue, is Henry Hohauser's outstanding Mediterranean-style building designed in 1936. It has a magnificent interior court with a four-sided gallery and balconies. The Parkway has been strikingly restored as rental apartments with Sender & Tragash as architects, and it is now known as the Place Vendome.

JEFFERSON AVENUE

850 Jefferson Avenue was designed by Henry Hohauser in 1939, and it is still in restoration. The paintwork beautifully articulates the sunrise relief and floral decoration in yellow, blue, and pink. A wave motif at the parapet delightfully emphasizes the curve.

940 Jefferson is a striking mixture of L. Murray Dixon's modernism and classicism. Black Vitrolite frames the entrance from which rises a central panel of louvered windows leading to a striking stepped parapet topped by a classical templetto. Designed in 1940.

Irma Siegel arrived from Chicago to do stage and interior design. She recalls putting on white gloves to shop there, and having your chauffeur drive you slowly down the street for window shopping. The stores were shaded by luxuriant palms and had the look of elegant French modernism. It was during the thirties that architects redesigned the Mediterranean-style facades to complement the new Deco hotels and movie theatres (there were three on Lincoln Road alone). Later, even before Bal Harbour became the major high-quality shopping center, and stores like Bonwit Teller, Lord & Taylor, and Macy's started to build in other south Florida locations, Morris Lapidus, the architect of the large new hotels to the north—the Fontainebleau and the Eden Roc—was selected to close Lincoln Road and design a mall. When MDPL in 1978 opened its headquarters in Dixon's former office just off the mall on Euclid, the Lincoln Road mall was in deep trouble. It was deserted and every other store seemed vacant.

At the City Planning Department various plans for revival and economic surveys grappled with the problem. Roofing over the mall with glass was a popular idea; turning the whole street into a central business district with high-rise housing backing up stores and offices was another. Lincoln Road became a white elephant for the city.

The revival of Lincoln Road in only the last few years is part of the original dream, combining a cultural approach with restoration of the Deco stores.

The solution is not total: it focuses on the west end of the mall, and in spite of the attention of the National Trust's Main Street experts, too many stores remain vacant. I believe that until Lincoln Road's potential as a Deco fashion center is fully developed, it never will be. Yet there has been a spectacular comeback based on a wedding of Art Deco restoration, art, and theatre. It has also proved to be an admirable example of the entire community putting itself behind a project. At the heart of the revival have been two elements: the South Florida Art Center, an aggregation of almost ninety artists and their studios, and twenty arts-related stores. The area that has enjoyed this revival is not the entire mall, but the blocks west of Meridian. Here the vacancies have dropped from forty percent in 1985, when the transformation began, to five percent at the present time.

The other element is the only Art Deco theatre of the thirties to have been restored: the Colony. Built in the mid-thirties, the theatre was considered a neighborhood theatre by its owners, Paramount Pictures, but because of its special location it has a rich history of premieres, such as the Ingrid Bergman film, *The Arch of Triumph.* A gift to the city in 1981

from Samuel Kipnis, a retired millionaire industrialist, the theatre after extensive remodeling now presents dance, films, and plays. The interior of the Colony was rebuilt with a stadium-type seating plan affording clear sightlines throughout the house. The carpeting is a reproduction of the carpeting in New York's Radio City Music Hall; the wood wainscoting and metal railings are original, but new lighting and acoustical systems help make the theatre a true contemporary multiuse facility. Across the street on Lincoln Road are the studios of a new ballet company, Miami City Ballet, directed by the noted dancer Edward Vilella. The Colony's combination of theatre, ballet, and artists have brought a new glamour to Miami Beach.

Club 1235—Disco Secret

It cost 5 million dollars when it was built in 1938 as a lavish supper club, the French Casino. It cost 5 million dollars to reopen the doors in 1984 as the ultimate nightclub—Z.

Although in its present incarnation as Club 1235 the old supperclub space still draws five thousand patrons each weekend to the District, to the average visitor to the Beach this one-time marvel of Art Deco is still unknown. A series of unfortunate decisions by the building's owners, the Brandts, have robbed it of its striking marquee and glass-block facade, so one now has to hunt to find the entrance and the place to purchase advance tickets. For its young devotees this adds perhaps to the lure of the club: harking back to the days of speakeasies.

Still existing, however, and as *Herald* staff writer Andres Viglucci saw it in 1984, the club is "a high tech marvel where laser beams criss-cross through the air, smoke billows in the floor and three miles of horseshoe-shaped metal tubing support a Star Wars light show that ascends and descends over frenetic dancers' heads."

The original French Casino had been a lavish place for the high art of entertainment when it opened. The noted theatre architect Thomas Lamb, whose movie palaces were strung across the country, designed the interior. When we MDPL preservationists were allowed free access to the space in 1978 as potential restorers, the original French Casino interior was still intact. We wandered through empty halls discovering the ponderous revolving stage, the dressing rooms upstairs, delighting in the great vivid mural of a Deco moon, and flicking on lights to see stars twinkle in the atmospheric ceiling, a feature of Deco theatres that simulated romantic evening skies. We noted the 300

MICHIGAN AVENUE

A Mayan-style fountain in front of a Michigan Avenue apartment.

1575 Michigan is a restored, lyrical Deco building with a streamlined balcony centered by a floral plaque. Designed by M. J. Nadel in 1936.

The Evelyn at 711 16th Street was designed by Gerald Pitt in 1936. The incised designs in the keystone name plaque above the entrance contrast effectively with the simplicity of the architectural massing emphasized by the blue-green striping.

16TH STREET

21ST STREET AREA

The Plymouth at 336 21st Street, by Anton Skislewicz, 1940, with a World's Fair–like pylon and drum-shaped tower, is a fascinating and unique structure. It was recently acquired as a headquarters for the New World Symphony, a gift from philanthropist Ted Arison. The Adams Hotel is in the background.

Period interior details from the circular lobby of the Plymouth, a very upper-class resort hotel in its time. Padded leather wall, cove lighting around the room, and a mural by Ramon Chatov of a semi-abstract tropical beach scene.

This is a detail photograph of the Adams tower, with its chamfered corners and deeply fluted concrete fence—an impressive architectural composition by L. Murray Dixon, 1938, that has been revivified with new colors by Jacqueline Yde, ASID.

pink seats and the swooping railings of the balcony. Theatre buffs told us that the acoustics ranked high among the best Deco theatres in the country.

Its design was actually quite simple despite the opulence of its interior. It had the clean sculptural look of later Deco. Its great effectiveness was in the curving walls, a high point in the plastering technique of Italian craftsmen that pioneer developer Carl Fisher brought to Miami, and in the series of boxes that formed descending arcs on either side.

The French Casino disappeared during World War II. Military-training films were shown there. The place never really recovered the glamour of the French Casino days, and after the war it became the Cinema Theatre, the name by which we knew it in the late seventies when we were trying to save it. Legions of Miamians grew up influenced by its special beauty as they sat watching the movies of the fifties and sixties.

The first time we went to the Cinema Theatre with a committee of designers, Andres Fabregas, who had joined the League in the first place because of his love for the movie theatre, remembered the gold-leafed columns in the lounge, so we peeled back mirrored tile to disclose the original gold. We discovered a name plate on the long snaking bar in the lounge—"Thonet," it said. Later, at that same ASID meeting in Washington where we saved the post office, I told the president of the Thonet furniture company about the bar. Clad in abalone shell, the bar often had been described as being veneered in mother of pearl. Behind it was another mural, an intricate orange-and-gold painting discovered by Carl Weinhardt, Jr., on that first survey day, when he climbed behind the bar and poked through rubbish.

In the interim before Club Z, while the Cinema had become a rallying cry for theatre-preservation buffs all over, the Brandts discussed converting it into a supermarket or tearing it down. I would have long conversations with their lawyer sons and Bingo Brandt, the father. "It can't make it as a movie theatre," he would say. "What old person in the neighborhood is going to come here? They are too poor."

The League, aware that there were seven theatres to be restored from the boom days of the past, wanted the Cinema to become a community theatre for concerts and other stage programs and cited the success of that great Art Deco monument, the Paramount Theatre, in Oakland, California. We succeeded in having the City Commission authorize a feasibility study and declare in favor of saving the Cinema.

In 1979, just before the first Art Deco Weekend, we were summoned from our office in the Cardozo and ran through the streets to pound on the barred door of the Cinema—a scene Miamians were to see on the six o'clock news, which emphasized the idea that preservation on the Beach was a battle. Wreckers had arrived and were destroying the facade so as to install a row of little shops. The Brandts' logic: to save the entire building they would need to get some income to pay taxes. This remodeling was to result in the removal of the grand staircase and its chrome railing and the taking down of the Deco chandelier.

When the Brandts announced that they had leased the theatre, we rejoiced and said that anything, even a disco, would be fine. Still knowing nothing of the demands and costs of discos, we were unprepared for what seemed a savage stripping of the interior.

Club Z opened with a press conference at city hall and nights of parties. Many of the treasures were gone. The restorers of Club Z had not allowed us in during the days of restoration, when they painted over the mural. "It would cost too much to restore water damage," and the red-and-pink color scheme of the mural was different from the one they intended to use in the club.

The 1980 uses for the Cinema—now Club 1235—constitute the "half-a-loaf" theory that characterizes much preservation around the country. With the chandeliers, grand staircase, and chrome railing restored, the coves glowing, and the iridescent bar in place, enough Deco quality remains to call this a Deco place and to attract the "Miami Vice" cameras on a regular basis. Hefty bar tabs and a $12 admission charge make the Club profitable enough to have insured its presence for a while. The Club has not become a supermarket, as was threatened for a long time; nor was it razed as so many Deco theatres have been. But on the other hand, what a potential for true splendor has been lost! A comparison with the Paramount Theatre in Oakland, across the bay from San Francisco, emphasizes what Miami Beach has forfeited. As a community theatre for concerts, symphonies, and theatrical events, the Oakland Paramount has prospered since 1976, and all its Deco treasures have been lovingly restored and maintained. This is also true of many theatres around the U.S.: the Fox in Atlanta, Georgia; the Paramount in Aurora, Illinois; the Fox in Spokane, Washington; and, of course, the most revered of all, the Radio City Music Hall in New York City, with its Deco furnishings collected and designed by Donald Deskey. Will the disco period pass? Can the Cinema ever be returned to its original glory? Or must we now be happy with the expansive cushioned dance floor and the ceiling heavy with state-of-the-art sound-and-light projection systems so that we can still enjoy the happy fantasy of the loge designs and the amazing ceilings in the lobbies done by the Italian plasterers?

The Cinema was to be the first of several nightclubs in the District attracting the "stay-up-late" young crowd; at least one, Club Nu, is also a fine restaurant. Nu (an Egyptian word) is the product of a local construction family, and fills the shell of a former landmark restaurant, the Embers. Almost entirely remodeled by Robert Bleemer, AIA, with tiers of seats facing a large bar and with a dance floor in a second room, it now provides a basic setting for what can only be described as "set" changes every six months. The Club opened with an Egyptian theme done in Deco style: a large Tutankhamen bust, pillars with hieroglyphics, and so forth. Dancers and waiters were appropriately costumed. The second theme was futurism, and again the motifs and constructions reflected Deco sources.

The 1235 building also housed what was to become the 30's Promenade in 1983, a mini-shopping center that had been a Kress store right up to 1982, when developer Ron Molko bought it and restored the keystone. The first large-scale District project to get a tax write-off, the 30's Promenade opened with great fanfare during Art Deco Weekend with exhibitions of the type of businesses that might come. The Promenade, acquired in 1986 by Tony Goldman, now houses MDPL and our Welcome Center and store financed with preservation gifts and Community Development grant money. It should become increasingly a center for defending the District and educating visitors The Welcome Center was Dr. Ernest Martin's major goal as president and then chairman of MDPL, a goal he set early on when, as president of The National Council of Economic Development Directors, he saw the importance of Welcome Centers in other preservation cities.

Collins—Imperiled and Unique

In the Deco District the future for Collins Avenue is clouded, particularly below 17th Street. Yet preservationists say that it is Collins Avenue, not famous Ocean Drive, that will determine the staying power of the District as an integrated, unique phenomenon.

Much of this realization comes from the threat to demolish the Senator Hotel on the corner of 11th and Collins, and two apartment buildings to the north. As is usually the case, the beauty of the Senator was recognized by the media, mainly *after* the threat of demolition came about. Photographs of its details— the etched glass windows, its quaint plaster pelicans, its tower and stripes and swimming pool with nautical railings—had appeared in countless national

publications. Yet until the demolition threat focused attention on it, the significance of Collins Avenue was not fully recognized by developers or by those who dine on the porches of Ocean Drive. "The Collins Avenue hotels are too small"—that statement is taken for granted. Even members of the MDPL board talked of allowing certain buildings on Collins to be demolished because "there are better examples of the style."

The current owners of the Art Deco Hotels—the Royale Group that owns the Cardozo, Carlyle, and the Victor—have declared that the property they own on Collins Avenue—the Senator Hotel and two apartments—must be used for a giant parking garage. The fear is that with a three-story parking garage as a base, they will then be free to erect a high rise that will allow a view of the ocean over their own small hotels on Ocean Drive, thereby probably destroying one of the chief assets of the small hotels. There was a stunned discovery by those who had ignored the politics of the past that the city with its weak historic ordinance would do nothing to prevent this from happening. A final effort was made by preservationists to change the ordinance to protect buildings from demolition in a city-designated historic zone. Although, however, this law was passed by the City Commission in the summer of 1987, it was thought not to protect the Senator. In February 1988, it was believed, even by Mayor Alec Daoud as he admitted in June, that the Senator could not be saved and that demolition might start any day. An unprecedented people's movement and frequent vigils on the porch of the Senator resulted in new activity by the city. In an atmosphere of relief and victory Mayor Daoud suggested that the Royale Group swap the Senator for municipal parking lots behind the Cardozo. However, subsequent Commission meetings revealed difficulties in effecting a clear title, for in June 1988 the hotels were declared in default to their mortgage company. At the present time the situation is in limbo. But whatever the outcome, the outpouring of affection for one small Deco hotel proved to be headline news, and the sight of the Senator and its tower were familiar newsfare.

There is today a new awareness of the meaning of the Senator, not only for its own intrinsic value (it was not even illustrated in earlier books about the District) but also because it is part of the fabric of interrelated buildings on Collins. The subject of "fabric" has been noted in other famous districts. To change the symmetry of the Vieux Carré of New Orleans, for instance, or buildings ringing such jewels as the parks in Savannah, Georgia, or a street of Colonial cottages in Salem, Massachusetts, is not even

The Governor, Hohauser's 1939 masterpiece at 435 21st Street, is considered a twin to the Cardozo. Note the streamlining, stainless steel canopy, bosses, flagpole standard, fluting, and reliefs. The Quality Inn chain, now franchising the Governor, has sensitively maintained its gardens and interior detail.

The Tyler, L. Murray Dixon, 1937, is at 430 21st Street and directly faces the Governor. The photograph expertly captures Dixon's handling of streamline curves and eyebrows offset by the strong blue and white verticals. Owner David Pearlson has restored most of 20th-21st Street block, including the Adams and the Collins Park, with unifying planting and a shared pool.

thinkable. But it is difficult for the new developers of the Art Deco District to think in this same way. In order to service the hotels on Ocean Drive they are prepared to sacrifice Collins, and let it become a parking street. They are willing to tear the fabric of Murray Dixon's singular vision: the line of spires and the curving corners with their faceted windows that march north from the Essex House to the Senator.

On both sides of the street from the Senator on south, Dixon's spirit carries the feeling from block to block. But on the east side particularly there is a repetition of the Senator's style with its faceted corner set off by keystone; the deep set porch with terrazzo floors; the upward-thrusting sign-ornamented spire lighted by neon and shining with polished steel; and the profusion of Art Deco ornaments—porthole windows, curving sunshades, etched glass, sparkling terrazzo: the whole panoply of little-hotel specialness devised just for these hotels.

It is ironic that Collins should be given over to the car, for in the Deco period it was a very pedestrian street. The hotels, with their inviting doors open to the breezy shade of the porches, had boutiques and dining rooms for the public. There were juice bars on the street, and seasonal visitors strolled along the hotel row greeting friends. Interestingly, in the same period that these small hotels were being developed, larger hotels—up to ten stories, which was the maximum height allowed—were being designed by the same architects in the area between Espanola Way and 17th Street. The hotels were built facing the ocean side, with their set-back curving driveways facing Collins. The St. Moritz (Dixon, 1939), the Sands (France, 1939), the New Yorker (Hohauser, 1940), the Royal Palm, and the recently demolished Poinciana provided their architects with the opportunity to develop modest-sized skyscrapers where massing and verticality ended in elaborate towers.

Continuing this trend past 17th Street (Lincoln Road), the buildings grew larger and perhaps even more fanciful in their towers and facade decorations. The Ritz-Plaza (Dixon, 1940) had a very industrial tower, a cylinder set on glass blocks and cubes, and on its facade long vertical striping. The Delano (Swartburg, 1947) contributed the most fanciful tower with fins on four sides, sort of an exotic Aztec headdress motif. The National (France, 1940) was topped with a silver dome set on Moorish arches. Dixon's design for the Raleigh in 1940, on a corner site, was perhaps the most streamlined of these taller hotels. Asymmetrical, it rounded the corners to the north with ribbon windows. The vertical stripes of pink block continued to the tower, decorated with a

stylish R monogram. On the ocean side Dixon designed a bathing pavilion in a streamlined little tower, like that of the Waldorf Towers, reminiscent of lighthouses along the coast.

These larger hotels on Collins were slow to be included in the Deco development scenario, but most of them now have new owners, and openings occur regularly in order to announce new Deco interiors and/or clubs or restaurants.

21st Street Returns—Deco Landmarks

A fashion designer from Montreal; an interior designer from Chicago; the former owner of a demolished fantasy hotel in Surfside (the Castaways) working with the Quality Inn chain; a musician who became a Beach tourist authority—this is the cast that in the summer of 1987 suddenly made 21st Street regain its importance as the center for some of the finest buildings by the original architects for Miami Beach.

While the lineup of wonderful hotels on Ocean Drive was still the major focus of the media in summer 1987 (the "Miami Vice" camera shooting there for the fourth year, a place in the August issue of *Fortune,* and almost daily exposure in the pages of the local press), clever and imaginative painting and plastering created a new awareness of the treasures on 21st Street. Suddenly, there is a new lineup emerging opposite the Bass Museum in John Collins Park. This group of hotels will certainly be photographed as much as those on Ocean Drive in the future.

Most important, perhaps, in the Deco Revival is David Pearlson's restoration of the Adams Hotel (Dixon, 1938), the first of the monuments on 21st Street, which is now being called "Heritage Way." The Adams is a triumph of integration of the streamlined style with its site. The building comes powerfully to the street line, and, like the Tyler next door and the Plymouth across the street, has all its landscaped area in back. The porches serve as public space in place of a lawn or front yard.

The Adams Tower, one of the most elaborate in the District, is chamfered in the Mayan manner of the buildings of San Francisco's Golden Gate International Exposition that opened in 1939. The Adams was a precursor to Dixon's Collins Avenue corner-towered buildings.

Like the Senator, Tiffany, and Tudor hotels of 1939, this hotel curves around the corner together with its generous terrazzo porch and large corner windows. All of its fine detail has been clarified by the color scheme designed by Jacqueline Yde, AID, a designer residing in Miami Beach, whose Chicago interiors

The Bass Museum of Art, 2121 Park Avenue, is in Collins Park, donated to the city by founding father John Collins. His grandson, Russell T. Pancoast, designed the building as the Miami Beach Library and Art Center in 1930. The keystone facade attests to the infatuation with the Mayan style in architecture. The detail photograph shows one of the three keystone bas reliefs by noted sculptor Gustav Bohland—a stylized pelican—and the handsome wrought-iron sidelights. Plans for expansion of the museum are being developed by Hardy, Holtzman, Pfeiffer, New York architects.

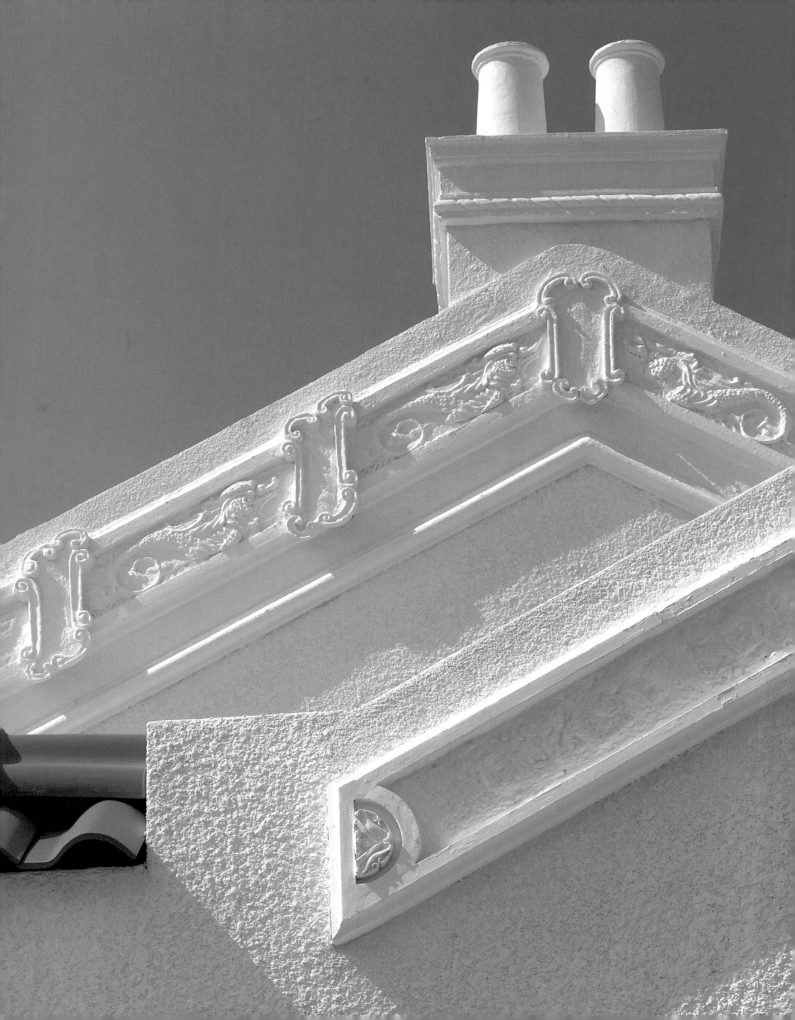

The National Register District boundaries make a jog at 21st Street and Washington Avenue to encompass the restored original clubhouse of the municipal golf course. Zyscovich & Grafton were the architects for the restoration, which brought out well the charm of the oldest building in Miami Beach, designed by August Geiger in 1916. A Florida architecture award went to the preservation architects. The detail photograph on the opposite page was featured on the cover of the 1986 issue of *Florida Architect*. Now used as a community center, the clubhouse includes a small theatre and a terrazzo dance floor.

The Collins Park at 2000 Park is another Hohauser marvel from 1939. Rippling wings lead to the circular entry, dramatized by vertical columns. The spandrels are decorated with a handsome chevron design.

The Abbey Hotel, 300 21st Street, designed by Albert Anis in 1940, with a tower reminiscent of those at San Francisco's Golden Gate International Exposition in 1939, has been stunningly restored by Canadian designer Mortimer Garflick, with color articulating Robert Swartburg's sculpture for the tower and the large and stylish flamingo plaque on the side at street level.

This detail photograph of the Collins Park Hotel dramatizes the beauty of the masterful facade over the entrance.

Chase Federal Savings and Loan, 1100 Lincoln Road, was designed by August Geiger in 1947, one of the last works of this master of the Federal Deco style. The double-eagle relief is an unusually good sculptural treatment of our national symbol. The doors are decorated with handsome chrome bosses, and a stepped metal pediment is set above.

The Colony Theatre, 1040 Lincoln Road, was built by Paramount, and designed by R. A. Benjamin in 1934. Reopened with a gala in 1976, it represents a major community effort. The original interior details were kept. Morris Lapidus, the noted planner for Lincoln Road mall and the Fontainebleau Hotel, was architect for the restoration.

have gained her much acclaim. The Tyler and Collins Park by Anis and Hohauser, respectively, are also an important part of the streamlined style in this block completed in 1939. David Pearlson has been planting palms and other trees compatible with the original plantings for the Governor Hotel across the street, which still survive from the forties. Pearlson's Heritage Café, which opened with a great party in the spring of 1988, uses the lobby and long porch of the Tyler as a Deco setting for French cuisine. The large windows reveal 21st Street as a leafy retreat.

The restoration of the Abbey on 21st Street by Mortimer Garflick, a relatively new hotelier from Montreal who was formerly a fashion designer, has brought a new charm to that hotel, which has been continuously in operation. Appropriate new wallpapers, carpeting, furniture in the lobby, and restyled rooms are pleasant, but it is the exterior of this 1940 hotel by Albert Anis that particularly delights. The corner tower, which according to muralist Paul Silverthorne, was sculpted in plaster by Robert Swartburg, is decorated with a relief sculpture of an alligator and flowers. On either side are decorative flagstaffs with tulip finials.

The Plymouth Hotel, of course, will always be one of the wonders of the District. Built in 1940, the same year as the Abbey, and designed by Anton Skislewicz, it is astonishingly reminiscent of the Trylon and Perisphere, the central symbol of the 1939-1940 New York World's Fair. Like that icon of the Deco world, the Plymouth features two impressive sculptural elements: a pylon towering over a rounded entry. If any one building epitomizes the abstract qualities of the architecture of the Deco period, this is it! This impressive central shape is the center from which wings flow on either side, and the whole is a powerful, unornamented study in concrete. The porch projects without a canopy, and like much of the interior lobby, it is made of white marble.

The Plymouth was the focus of our initial rallies during the first summer when it was boarded up, the place from which we called for lights and action to the delight of the press. When the National Register directors came down to see our District that was creating such excitement, they too met the press on the marble porch of the Plymouth, and stayed across the street at the Governor.

The Plymouth, however, has still not been restored. Yet it was the first we considered. Arquitectonica partner Laurinda Spear did renderings of how the lobby might be restored. The lobby had contained a café in the palmy days when *House & Garden* called it one of Miami's most elegant hotels, and when limousines pulled up to the side door. The walls were covered with quilted leather, which is still there but painted over in white. The counter of the registration desk, like the one at the Abbey, was made of marble with a Regency swag design. The café area leads to a lovely pool lined in keystone. The Plymouth is still waiting for someone to refurbish its elegant interior, which now seems more likely, for the Plymouth was purchased by shipping magnate Ted Arison as a residence hotel for the New World Symphony, a well-supported orchestra of young musicians.

Across the street the Governor, almost a duplicate of the Cardozo, dominates the street. It is amazing to think that Hohauser could not only produce the Governor and Cardozo in the same year, 1939, but also the Collins Park, another wonderful building that stands on 20th Street and shares a courtyard with the Adams and the Tyler. The Governor is built right to the edge of the street, and one's eye is entranced by a series of decorative flourishes: the door with its ornamental Deco grille, the etched glass, the plaques with abstract wave designs, the curved steel canopy and steel bosses, and flagstaff. This is one of Hohauser's great achievements, a triumph of horizontality that sweeps around to the garden on the east. The interior is fully as striking with a brass elevator door, ziggurated arches, and terrazzo. The Quality Inn, the first national hotel chain to operate a Deco hotel in the District, has treated this fine building with respect. A pleasant coffee shop has been installed, and there is additional dining space on the porch. Pianists and violinists from the New World Symphony down the street at the Plymouth play at the cocktail hour in the refurbished lobby, and outdoor dining is available in the garden courtyard. The rooms, with Deco fabrics and paintings, have been brought up to national standards, and a parking lot is well concealed by trees and hedges. Entering from the side door, you see a moving electric sign with the message "Welcome to the Governor, gem of the Art Deco District, designed by Henry Hohauser in 1939." Clearly, the Art Deco District is sending out a signal to middle America.

Twenty-first Street grows increasingly interesting. To the east is the beginning of the boardwalk; to the west is Washington Avenue with the sensitive restoration of an old clubhouse that is now the community center; and a new community center and a very large convention center are now being built. There is a new paved walk along the street, leading from Washington to the boardwalk. There is Wolfie's, a restaurant that is a sturdy ally to the district through the Nevel family; its Celebrity Room has portraits of the stars who used to come to the Beach. There is the 21st Street library, which was taken over in 1986 by

The expert restoration of the Sterling Building has brought this office and shop building back to beautiful life. The Sterling was designed by Alexander Lewis in 1928, with a redesign in 1941 by V. H. Nellenbogen. Architectural preservation work was by Carlos Marin, AIA, in 1986. The new wrought-iron door and buffed terrazzo symbolize the sophistication of this complete restoration.

Two shots of the Sterling Building at dusk. The wonderful restoration was funded by the Wolfson Foundation. The expert handling of the lighting was done by Carlos Marin, AIA. The building now houses the Foundlings, a private women's club.

The Lincoln Cinema building at 555 Lincoln Road was designed by Robert E. Collins between 1935 and 1936. Its parapet is a veritable cascade of floral bas-relief ornament. Thomas Lamb, noted for his movie-palace designs, was responsible for the interior, owned by Wometco and unrestored.

The Albion Hotel at 1650 James Avenue, with shops and entrances on Lincoln Road, was designed by Igor Polevitsky in 1939. Some have called it an example of Nautical Moderne because of its fins, seen as smokestacks, and prominent portholes. An elaborate urban hotel with gardens and pool, it could be restored to great effect.

the county and which is being readied to house a major Art Deco collection.

Finally, there is the Bass Museum, originally designed by Russell T. Pancoast. The 1988 exhibition called "Miami Commercial Architecture" at the museum showed an early rendering of the wonderful keystone entrance, and over the doors is a wrought-iron sign proclaiming that the building was both a *library* and an *art center*. The misinformation that has been flourishing concerning our recent past states that the building served only as a library in its pioneering days. Recent archival finds by the director of the museum, Diane Camber, reveal a vibrant intellectual community centering around the Miami Beach Library and Art Center, a place that helped fuel the intellectual ferment that resulted in Miami's sophisticated buildings. The gallery space on the second floor, which is currently used for special exhibits, was a gallery right from the beginning. The first exhibition, organized by Mrs. Thomas Pancoast, the architect's mother, showed the work of Arthur Dove, the distinguished American abstract painter. A later exhibit was devoted to Lessing Rosenwald's print collection. Beach artist Fred Albert recalls that when he was a student at the University of Miami in the fifties, classes regularly went to the Art Center.

In 1964, when John Bass gave his collection to the city, the museum was renamed, and the current library was built at Collins and 21st. Robert Swartburg was the architect for the renovation. In 1980, the city took over the museum, and Carl Weinhardt, Jr., did much to bring the interior back to its thirties splendor, including having banners and logotype designed that incorporated as a motif the abstract seagulls on the cornices of the building.

The stage was set for Diane Camber, whom the city appointed as director of the museum, to raise its sights and make it once again the cultural center of the city and of the Art Deco District. Regular concerts, exhibitions, films, and lectures give substance to the study of the fine arts of the twentieth century. In 1986, the museum won formal accreditation from the American Association of Museums, for it passed with flying colors such criteria as its educational program, the care accorded its growing collection, cataloguing, and most of all, the splendid exhibitions that have brought thousands of people into the District.

Now the museum is confidently pursuing an expansion program, following initial plans made by the New York architects Hardy Holtzman Pfeiffer and Associates. New wings for the museum will provide 68,000 square feet for storage, research, and other needs. Diane Camber, who has already raised considerable funds, believes that the museum will become the true cultural center for the Art Deco District.

The Magic Imagery of Miami Beach

Every election year on Miami Beach—every second year, that is—candidates swear "I love Miami Beach!" In truth, however, they appear to have been ashamed of it for some time. As a matter of fact, in summer 1987 a publicist suggested that Miami Beach should be called "Oceanside" to cash in on the new popularity of Bayside, the Rouse shopping development across the water.

Our own experiences have shown, however, how powerful a hold the Miami Beach of the recent past has had on the American imagination. In 1980 my son Andrew commissioned Woody Vondracek to do a poster for the Cardozo. Woody drew a rough sketch and we asked a newly married couple to pose for it. She borrowed her mother's old dress, he found a fedora. Woody placed them on the keystone balustrade of the Cardozo porch, and the great image he titled "Come Back to the Sea" was born. The poster subsequently appeared in *The New Yorker* (one of the first tiny hotel institutional ads now such a commonplace) and in several city magazines: *New York, Chicago, Washington.*

A massive attempt was made by the little hotel group on Miami Beach to become highly visible at tourism conferences and at Art Deco Society Weekends, like the one Chicago held on a Great Lakes Deco dayliner. In tourist offices everywhere the poster brightened display windows. I remember the impact seeing it displayed in Illinois in suburban Highland Park's exclusive shopping street one cold Chicago winter.

The poster promised not only fond memories of an elegant past but also the sun and beauty of a tropical beach. There began to be a steady flow of visitors—not only from outposts like Alaska and Japan and Buenos Aires—but also from all over the U.S. People came to us who were reliving honeymoons, and childhood trips, and stints on the Beach during the war. Miami Beach, like Saratoga, Atlantic City, Timberline, Asheville, and the other places we reviewed in our 1984 conference, "America's Great Historic Resorts," had a franchise no one could take away. It was beloved by the world as a happy, pleasant place, and all sorts of people from all sorts of places were rooting for us.

The city of Miami is a changed place from only a decade ago when we would cross McArthur Causeway and see only the Freedom Tower and the county courthouse on the horizon. How significant it is that the Freedom Tower is now all but obscured in today's skyline, and it is still in need of rehabilitation. Millions of dollars have gone into the new world of Miami. Preservation is certainly more difficult than razing and building new buildings. But memory and image are strong, and the reality of the hard, impersonal big downtown has not penetrated to the rest of the world. Despite "Miami Vice," riots, a changed constituency, and thriving multinational business, "Miami" to many people still means the image Woody Vondracek conjured up in 1980: a girl and a guy under a palm tree at the water's edge.

The Uncertain Future: Preservation vs. Development

In 1980, two top-ranking officials from HUD came down from Washington to visit us. They crowded into my tiny office in the MDPL headquarters, which originally had been L. Murray Dixon's offices. They represented not only the big money that the Carter administration was putting into rebuilding cities but also an understanding of what was going on in real estate nationally and the scope of what could eventually happen. The meeting was the result of intense lobbying in Washington and long phone calls. The gentlemen from HUD were our lifeline to public spending that could turn our dreams into reality. What they said that morning to our staff and to our attorneys was to echo in my ears for a long time after. "You will never make it," they concluded. "Development is marching southward all along the coast from Jacksonville. The best and highest use of the land is seen as high rises—condominiums. There is no waterfront left to build on; yours is the last pocket. What you have achieved is miraculous in the face of this relentless trend. But it is doomed. You don't have the money or the political clout to survive. Everyone in Washington would like to help you, but the government is reluctant to go into situations where there is so much controversy."

Basically, the drama of the Art Deco District remains the struggle between development growth and preservation development. To the immediate south of the District is the area we have deserted, which is between Fifth Street and the island's tip where Government Cut meets the ocean. With the exception of Joe's Stone Crab restaurant, which has prospered during the ten years of District rebirth, the area has been slowly emptied of its population. Buildings have been demolished, picked off one by one. For five years a moratorium prohibited restoration, and the poor and criminal population that took over the area made it unsafe. Other previous

Beach landmarks—the greyhound racetrack, the pier, the Coast Guard house—all have disappeared. The city took over, named the area South Pointe, and spent millions of dollars on sewers and roads. In 1987 we saw the opening of the first condominium tower, softened with a coat of Deco pink.

After a period of ejecting the elderly, condemning buildings, planning, surveying, and promoting the area as the city's most exciting location, fate dealt South Pointe an ironic blow in the summer of 1987. Two small hotels, the 1937 Savoy Plaza and the Arlington, were purchased by a European investment company headed by Ron Wood, the lead guitarist of the Rolling Stones. A large resort club has been developed there, and its facade is a vision in new glass block and pastel neon. The old buildings proved to have more appeal for recycling than vague plans for new buildings. Suddenly, this has become the hot new investment area. In spite of the elaborate plans to treat it as "raw land" and erect new buildings, it is the 1920s and 1930s buildings that are being sold. A new evironmental group is defending the remaining waterfront-park space.

Meanwhile, almost every issue of the local papers carries stories heralding "Success for Art Deco." Large hotel chains, mostly known for their economy rates, have purchased real estate in the District so as to upgrade their image. Days Inn will build a new 220-room complex and tower in "Deco and Post-Modern style," but are demolishing the 1939 Bancroft and the Jefferson to do so. Quality Inn, as we have already noted, purchased the Governor on 21st Street and installed a parking lot and a café. Holiday Inns owns the large hotel on Washington and 22nd Street and are actively at work refurbishing and promoting their District property. Much of this is seen as a response to opportunities to be provided by the multimillion-dollar expansion of the Convention Center.

Even the beach itself is not safe from overdevelopment. A new restaurant to be built on the sand, a branch of Penrod's of Fort Lauderdale, has been given a long lease by the city.

The plan, the harmony, developed by that small group of gifted young architects in the thirties is disappearing before our eyes. In our early days of forecasting the future of the District, we discussed the necessity for development, for rebuilding with hidden infill not seen from the street, and perhaps rashly, the need to erect new buildings that represented the thinking of contemporary architects rather than simply copying the thirties style.

But the District preservationists now are despairing that these ideas about development may end in the loss of the older buildings. We have come to a new

SURROUNDING
THE DECO DISTRICT

The boundary makers for the District in 1978 considered their decisions to be somewhat arbitrary, as so many monuments lay to the south and north. Here are some favorite examples. The District influence is constantly spreading north to the homes designed by the District's architects in the late thirties—including Pancoast, Geiger, Dixon, and Hohauser.

This moongate at the J. J. Astor estate on Pine Tree Drive, set in a keystone wall with Deco ornamentation, is a beautiful example of Deco craftsmanship in wrought iron. Other gates on Pine Tree Drive are Mayan in inspiration, also using keystone.

Roy Lichtenstein's *Mermaid* sculpture, funded by Art in Public Places, stands in front of the Lapidus-designed Center for the Performing Arts. The sculpture of this world-famous artist includes pieces inspired by Deco forms.

The Flamingo Apartments at 2460 Flamingo Drive were designed by L. Murray Dixon in 1940 and have been wonderfully restored in Deco Revival style.

The Helen Mar Apartments, now condominiums, are the most ambitious recycling program north of the District. Designed by Robert E. Collins in 1936 for John Marsa, contractor, the building was restored by architect Yossi Friedman of New York. The black Vitrolite striping and bas reliefs contribute importantly to the stylishness of the whole. The building is effectively illuminated at night and seen across Lake Pancoast from Collins Avenue.

Deco Plaza, a reconstruction of the sorely deteriorated MacArthur Hotel at 5th Street and Euclid and designed by T. Hunter Henderson in 1920, was redeveloped as a consortium between a private developer and a raft of city and county bureaus. It is a design triumph for Leonard Horowitz, for it transforms the street with bright color and has stimulated other retail and club activity on 5th Street. The ziggurat-shaped capitals with floral detail are a delight, and the raised passageway (shown at the bottom of the opposite page), painted with couples in period costume, is a true imaginative touch.

realization of the worth of the District as a true museum of twenties and thirties architecture, to be as carefully preserved as the historic districts of Annapolis or Charleston.

Massive public and private expenditure is now needed to preserve and intensify the authentic Art Deco experience. Our hotels must glitter once more; the spirit of the jazz and streamlined decades must be reborn. Interiors should again be sleek and glamorous with deep-cut carpeting, tubular chrome, exciting illumination, and authentic paintings and sculpture from the period. We need the tropical planting, the bright beach umbrellas, the languor and intimacy the neighborhood once had. If this seems economically impossible, if we cannot rise to the challenge, the conclusion is inevitable. These may well be the last days to experience the genius created by Hohauser, Dixon, and their peers.

T. D. Allman in his wonderful book *Miami: City of the Future* pokes what might be described as affectionate fun at the dreamers of Miami—those who have gambled everything on their dreams, brought the city their money and their energy, and then departed or died with nothing tangible to show. Allman counts me among the dreamers, comparing me to Julia Tuttle, the famous pioneer of Miami Beach, and he scoffs at my sons and at me because we thought the District could work in many contradictory ways at the same time—as a place for the young and affluent and as a haven for the old and poor.

Some say—and I have been guilty of it—that what we need is a billionaire who will take the whole District over, impose controls, and make it work. In our minds, of course, is John D. Rockefeller, Jr.'s Williamsburg restoration, where cars and parking are at the gates and not in the Colonial settlement; where costumed actors and working craftsmen simulate America before the Revolution; where neat, regulated inns, shops, and restaurants are on the periphery of the restored area, and celebrations take place inside on the quaint streets and greens both day and night, winter and summer.

This Disneyland approach to the District is tempting: the slums would disappear along with their inhabitants; jazz and Big Band music would be in the air; the cars lined up along the curbs would be Cords and early Buicks. Hotel interiors would approach museum quality: furniture would have veneers of rare woods or would be reproductions of machine-age styles by Kem Weber and Donald Deskey. The colors of the building facades would conform to one another, harmonizing gently. Miami Beach, newly re-created as it was when all who knew it still describe it as a "paradise," would mean tropical flowers and trees, birds and fountains, organ grinders with monkeys, plentiful juice bars, awning-shaded verandahs, and pennants flying again from all the chrome masts. It might also be possible to replace today's black asphalt with the white concrete roads that set off the bright buildings so much better, and perhaps also coat them lightly with sand as happened naturally in the early days.

This is, of course, pre-"Miami Vice" thinking: the District is not and probably never could be a trim, unreal monument to the past, however pleasant that might be. It will never have a scrubbed, "squeaky-clean" atmosphere with controlled crowds and events. The Beach, like it or not, has become the flashy, adventurous, and permissive reality of the world-famous TV series.

It has also become a place for impromptu entertainment, for hanging out, for conversation and affairs, for being as sand-covered and damp as you can get at the beach and as cool and elegant as you can be when you arrive in a stretch limousine to enter Club Nu. It has developed into a place for individuality in business ventures as well as in costume. Here is where you finally get to own—and lose—that small hotel, or to open the boutique where you indulge your passion for hats or far-out art.

Encouraging hotel chains to provide adequate housing for large conventions and plenty of rooms with an ocean view (at the expense of someone else's view) may work for the property owners, but it will surely kill the casual individualism of the present District. The new ventures now proposed will also destroy what is nostalgic and fragile in the District.

The way to make the Art Deco District work and live is to respect what's here—the small, beautiful, and resourceful buildings—and to understand what they were, and to bring them back to glamorous life, using all the technology and all the financing one would need to destroy them and then build some giant nightmare of a building in their place.

The second wave of developers, the youngsters who are today serving dinners and parking cars, selling real estate, and preserving Florida's reputation for beautiful, healthy people, don't know or care very much about the history of the beautiful buildings in this book. But if they put up a good fight to keep what they've got here in unique Miami Beach, they too will come to respect the original architectural team that made the District possible and the modern movement in the arts of which our architects were such a significant part. Meanwhile, our visitors—the wonderful, responsive, educated visitors who know and deeply appreciate what they are seeing—will join us in safeguarding and enjoying the Art Deco architecture in our beautiful Miami Beach.

Because of its southernmost location in South Pointe the photogenic little Century Hotel at 140 Ocean Drive is often considered an early example forecasting future Miami Beach architecture. Actually, however, it is one of Henry Hohauser's 1939 fantasies, deriving its main impact from the concrete mast with fins that rises above the entrance.

BIBLIOGRAPHY

Agee, William C. *The 1930's Painting and Sculpture in America.* Catalog for October-December exhibit, Whitney Museum of American Art, New York, 1968.

Arwas, Victor. *Art Deco.* New York: Harry N. Abrams, 1980.

Aslet, Clive. "Stepped Back and Laid Back", *Country Life,* March 12, 1987, 94, 95.

Bartlett, Ellen. "Miami Beach Bets on Art Deco." *Historic Preservation,* January-February 1981, 9–13.

Bletter, Rosemarie H. and Cervin Robinson. *Skyscraper Style: Art Deco New York.* New York: Oxford University Press, 1975.

Capitman, Barbara Baer, ed. *Time Present, Time Past.* Florida Endowment for the Humanities project, Miami, 1979.

Capitman, Barbara Baer, ed. *Portfolio: The Art Deco Historic District.* Photographs by David Kaminsky. Funded by the National Endowment for the Arts, Bill Bucolo (publisher), Miami, 1980.

Cerwinske, Laura. *Tropical Deco: The Architecture and Design of Miami Beach.* Photographs by David Kaminsky. New York: Rizzoli, 1981, rep. 1987.

Cockburn, Alexander. "The Planned Destruction of Old Miami Beach." *The Village Voice,* April 27, 1982.

Duncan, Alastair. *American Art Deco.* New York: Harry N. Abrams, 1986.

Goldberger, Paul. *The Skyscraper.* New York: Alfred A. Knopf, 1983.

Greer A., and Nora Richter, eds. *Architecture, the AIA Journal* (December 1983): 34–68.

Grief, Martin. *Depression Modern: The 30's Style in America.* New York: 1975.

Hatton, Hay. *Tropical Splendor: An Architectural History of Florida.* New York: Alfred A. Knopf, 1987.

Hillier, Bevis. *The World of Art Deco.* New York: E. P. Dutton & Co., 1971.

"Historic Districts: The Washington Avenue Revitalization Program". *Progressive Architecture* (1982): 89–96.

Ingle, Marjorie. *Mayan Revival Style: Art Deco Mayan Fantasy.* Layton, Utah: Peregrine Smith, 1984.

Johnson, Carol Newton. *Tulsa Art Deco: An Architectural Era, 1925-1941.* Tulsa, Oklahoma: the Junior League of Tulsa Publications, 1980.

Liebs, Chester H. *Main Street to Miracle Mile: American Roadside Architecture.* New York: Little, Brown & Company, 1985.

Liss, Robert. "Deco Mania," *The Miami Herald Tropic Magazine,* 11 February, 1979, 18–23.

Menten, Theodore. *The Art Deco Style.* New York: Dover Publications, 1972.

Olson, Arlene R. "A Guide to the Architecture of Miami Beach." Miami Dade Heritage Trust, Miami, 1978.

Perrault, John. "Report from Miami." *Art in America,* November 1981: 51–56.

Poulos, Arthur J. *American Design Ethic: A History of Industrial Design to 1940.* Cambridge: Massachusetts Institute of Technology Press, 1983.

Rodriguez, Ivan A. *From Wilderness to Metropolis: The History and Architecture of Dade County, Florida, 1825-1940.* Metro Dade Office of Community & Economic Development, Historic Preservation Division, Miami, 1982.

Root, Keith. *Art Deco Guide.* Miami Design Preservation League, Miami Beach, 1987.

Rothman, et al., *Miami Beach Art Deco District: Time Future.* Based on the 1981 Anderson Natter Finegold study. Community Action and Research, Miami, 1981.

Scott-Brown, Denise. "My Miami Beach." *Interview,* August 1986.

Stone, Susannah Harris. *The Oakland Paramount.* Berkeley, California, 1981.

Vlack, Don. *Art Deco Architecture in New York, 1920-1940.* New York: Harper & Row, 1974.

Webb, Michael. *Hollywood Legend and Reality.* Published in conjunction with Smithsonian Institution Traveling Exhibition Service, April 1986 to February 1987. Boston: Little, Brown & Company, 1986.

Weber, Eva. *Art Deco in America.* New York: Exeter Books, 1985.

Wilson, et al. *The Machine Age in America.* The Brooklyn Museum traveling exhibition. New York: Harry N. Abrams, 1986.